Borderline Hardy in 5b

the improbable success of
Pleasant Valley Nurseries

Bruce Partridge

with a foreword by
Henri Steeghs

© 2021 Bruce Partridge

All rights reserved. No part of this book may be reproduced or transmitted in any form or by any means, electronic or mechanical, including photocopying, or by any information storage or retrieval system, without permission in writing from the publisher.

Cover: Rebekah Wetmore, from an image by Henri Steeghs
Editor: Andrew Wetmore

ISBN: 978-1-990187-07-0
First edition June, 2021

397 Parker Mountain Road
Granville Ferry NS
B0S 1A0

moosehousepress.com
info@moosehousepress.com

We live and work in Mi'kma'ki, the ancestral and unceded territory of the Mi'kmaq People. This territory is covered by the "Treaties of Peace and Friendship" which Mi'kmaq and Wolastoqiyik (Maliseet) People first signed with the British Crown in 1725. The treaties did not deal with surrender of lands and resources but in fact recognized Mi'kmaq and Wolastoqiyik (Maliseet) title and established the rules for what was to be an ongoing relationship between nations. We are all Treaty people.

Foreword

If one would wish to coax a living from making the world a more beautiful place, there's no better way than using plants to do so. This beautiful province seemed to me, a young and eager immigrant, like a lovely and most suitable place to put this idea into practice.

Without my knowing about hardpans or perched water tables, thus began a long and trying journey learning about the heavy clay soils of Northeastern Nova Scotia and becoming acquainted with flash freezes and the general lack of spring.

But if the choice of location was my calvary, the people who joined in made up for it, and much of my (or PVN's) good fortune rests with the plant-lovers who came onboard to be a part of it all.

When Bruce first joined the team, I quickly noticed his keen power of observation and his steady eye for things. Before the workday began, he'd comment on the way the season had advanced—and changed the colour or the shape of twigs or buds—since yesterday.

We spent long hours debating the benefits of "feeding" plants and deliberating on apple rootstocks. And gradually we realized that nature's brilliant ways of arranging her plants outdid our most sincere attempts, and decided that that was worth a closer look.

Over time we journeyed through deep woods, across bogs and over cliffs to observe the wilderness and look for fine examples of rare plants and nature's noble ways.

One such trek, pursuing the elusive fragrant fern, took us over steep and inaccessible terrain (in Guysborough County) to a hidden waterfall where, just below the spray, mosses and ferns of every description hung from the rocks, appearing as unconcerned as on the first day of creation.

Plant-finding missions like this led us to many other special places in Northeastern Nova Scotia and Cape Breton and eventually resulted in a short film that we made (*Treasures of the Old*

Forest, which you can find on YouTube) in order to give greater thought to forest harvest practices.

On the job, Bruce was not only known for his insights, but for his talents as a natural storyteller. Sensible in all regards, he excelled at dispensing useful plant and garden knowhow and saw the humour in our human ways. A patient and good listener, he made people feel okay about their own (gardening) mistakes and was respected by staff and customers alike. Able to extract some comedy from the everyday, he often made us laugh, which helped to keep our spirits up through difficult or trying times when plant losses, unforeseen expenses or weeks of bad weather would nearly cause us to lose faith.

Our fickle "seasonal" business model managed to survive through the uncertain times by virtue of the steady hand of Phyllis, my wife and partner, who handled multiple departments, gave everyone a voice and sometimes performed miracles to keep the ship afloat.

In winter months, we propagated plants and ran the business from our home. My sons grew up in the greenhouses, unloading trucks between the planting jobs, and realized all jobs are urgent at a nursery.

The people at PVN came from every walk of life and everywhere on the map. Our varied backgrounds, coupled with the love of plants, made for a rich and generous connection between us all as four decades came and went. We may not have been saving lives, but we relished and taught the possibilities of dazzling flowerbeds and handsome trees, and luscious big tomato plants with aromatic fruit.

Bruce saw and understood the grace and beauty in plants and in people, both in their natural and cultivated ways. It was our privilege and joy to share this vision with this remarkable unselfish fellow man.

Henri Steeghs

Henri Steeghs in 1973, at the start of the adventure

To Pete Stovell and Bruce Davidson, comrades fallen too soon, whose spirit lives on as alive as yours or mine.

PVN 1978: (front, l-r) Bruce Partridge, **Bruce Davidson**, *Henri Steeghs, (back, l-r)* **Pete Stovell**, *Phyllis Baker, Frank Campbell*

Anna Syperek's lovely sketch on the PVN catalogue cover

Contents

Foreword..3
Introduction..11
The dream..17
The move to town...27
The landscaping years..35
The nursery...57
The greenhouses..67
The store..81
What we had going for us...113
The team...131
Gardening essays...135
    PVN tackles clay and rock..137
    Planting a tree...143
    Shade trees...148
    Fruit trees..153
    Nut trees..161
    Small fruits..170
    Site selection..180
    Flowering shrubs..186
    Evergreens..191
    Perennials...198
    Wildflower gardening..201
    Vegetable gardening..206
    Starting seeds...214
    Saving seeds..219
    Lawns..224
    Invasive plants..231
The back of the book..243
    Acknowledgements..245
    About the author...247

Bruce Partridge

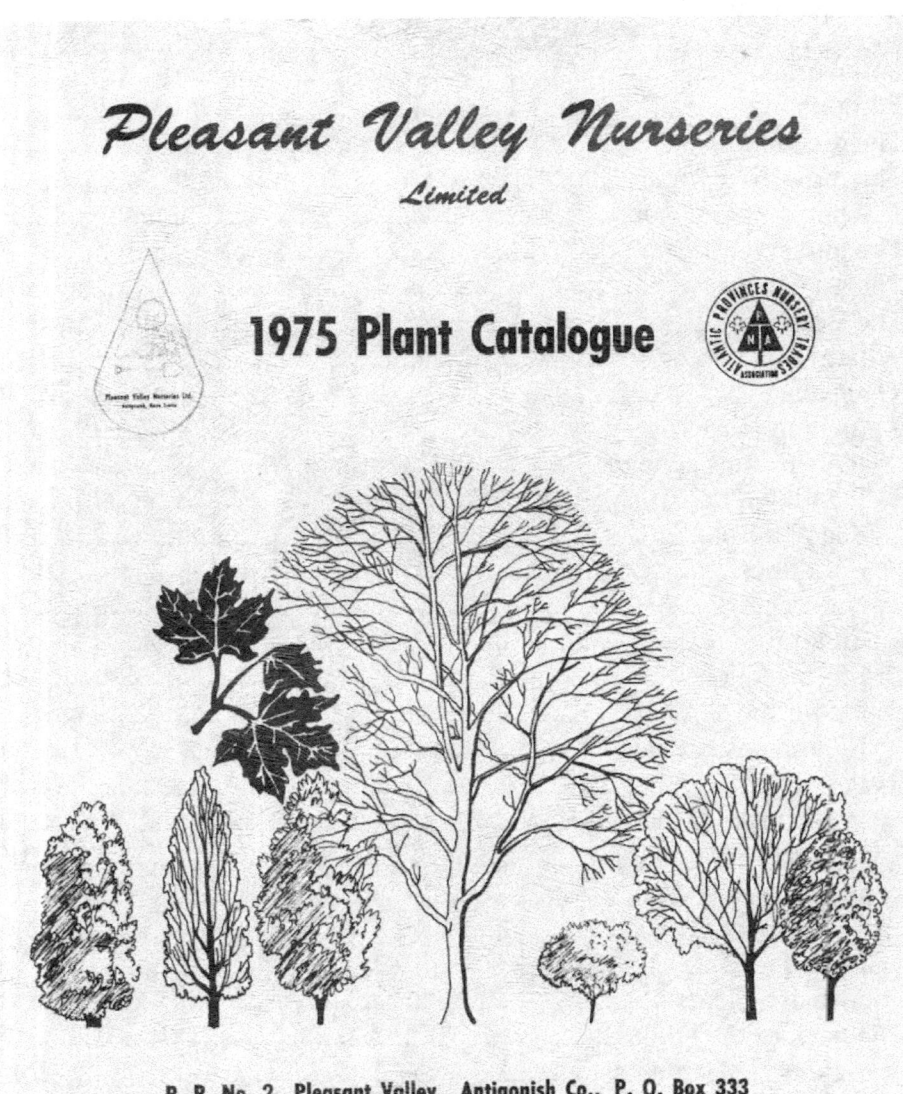

Our very first catalogue.

Introduction

Cars had been gathering for an hour, parked behind the chain and lined up on both sides of the Church Street Extension. Abandoning their vehicles, a crowd milled at the gate, hesitant to cross. In the distance, workers hurried back and forth, clutching clipboards and conferring in worried groups.

At 9 o'clock, a young helper went to open the chain. Shoulder to shoulder, like an advancing army, the rollicking mob surged down the drive. And then they were upon us.

The magnolias went first, then the rhododendrons and Japanese maples. Flowering dogwood, Spirea, Weigela, Quince and Forsythia went fast. Antigonish had never seen anything like it. The May 1, 2017 Pleasant Valley Nurseries going-out-of-business sale had begun.

From the opening of the chain until closing, gardeners picked up trees, shrubs and perennials, sometimes queuing up for an hour or more to get to the cash. No one lost their temper—spirits were high and the day was warm. There were no fights and no fender-benders. A peaceful demonstration if there ever was one.

But who were all these people? Men and women, young and old; children, even. Many we knew but others we did not. Bargain hunters? How come they were so happy and relaxed? Slowly it dawned on us. These people had gathered—to find bargains, yes—but mostly to pay tribute to the little small-town garden centre that had bucked hard times and fierce competition for over four decades, succumbing only to time and age. We were touched.

A fixture in Antigonish, Nova Scotia, Pleasant Valley Nurseries (PVN) in its 44 years carved a niche among gardeners all out of proportion to its size. PVN was a plant business—not a hardware store or a building-supply or a grocery. We, the staff, were enthusiastic plant people, trained in Ornamental Horticulture and Plant

Bruce Partridge

Science through the N.S. Agriculture College in Truro, doing what we loved. What we loved was gardening, discovering new plants, and sharing our knowledge and expertise with customers.

Gardeners recognized this and made PVN their destination for seeds, plants and advice. Some knew us all by name and looked for the one they liked to work with. It is impossible to overstate the pleasure we took in serving and getting to know avid gardeners from around the Maritimes. It was their enthusiasm and loyalty that kept us going all those years.

Throughout, PVN grew or brought in just about everything that could be grown in this climate. We imported introductions developed every year at experimental farms, research stations and commercial nurseries, but also remained true to old-fashioned favourites and native species. We were always there to advise on planting and culture, which kept customers coming back.

I don't think that it's an exaggeration to claim that Pleasant Valley Nurseries transformed ornamental gardening in this part of Nova Scotia, introducing plants and principles of design as taught in the brand-new program of Landscape Horticulture at the Agricultural College in Truro. Until PVN came along, planting in Antigonish County had been rather hit or miss, with most plants purchased through the mail.

We were young and evangelical and promoted the concept of combining trees and shrubs in larger beds. To make things easier, we offered a landscape planning service, and, if you needed one, a hard-working planting crew. Our raised beds had people looking.

Also, we were selling the right plants for this climate. The whole concept caught on, and homeowners began enthusiastically keeping up with the Joneses. At Pleasant Valley Nurseries they were sure to find that plant that they just absolutely had to have. Today when I drive around, I see attractive plantings everywhere that I know were inspired by our example.

Our greenhouses rode the crest of an awakening among Canadians for beautiful planters and hanging baskets to decorate their homes. Our team in the greenhouses outdid themselves each year with imaginative arrangements of summer blooms and colourful foliage, which were in great demand. Appreciative customers frequently brought back last year's empty containers for a professional refill. For many years, the town of Antigonish decorated with our hanging baskets and planters, and was honoured with awards from Communities in Bloom.

Pleasant Valley Nurseries was a popular place to visit. The greenhouses overflowing with flowers, trees and shrubs in every direction, well-established plantings, and a splashing pond gave the place the air of a botanical garden. Our customers, young and old, were loyal, and we gained new ones every year.

Interest in gardening continued to snowball and gardeners became steadily more sophisticated and skilful. We were delighted to introduce new plants, and to stay on top of new techniques and information. We printed a catalogue. Larger businesses attempted to sell plants and undercut our prices, but in the areas of experience, advice, and an extensive selection of plants, we had no competition.

In 2010 we joined the chosen in the May edition of *Canadian Gardening Magazine* as one of the twenty best garden centres in Canada. "Great stock for a relatively small place," they said.

We were indeed a relatively small place, but to be small in Antigonish—a very special little town—suited us fine. The journey to this heady plateau was a long one. Here is how it began:

The year is 1973. Pierre Trudeau is Prime Minister. It is the era of hitch-hikers, draft dodgers, long hair and Youth Initiative grants. Young people, flexing their wings, crisscross the country from B.C. to Nova Scotia or Newfoundland and back again, a good many washing up in Antigonish. Many stay.

In an old farmhouse in Pleasant Valley, Henri Steeghs sits one evening with some buddies. The boys are young—early twenties—mostly long-haired and bearded, most from away. Candles flicker. Neil Young music pounds out from big speakers: *Cinnamon Girl*. Some smoke or drink beer.

They are waiting for the phone to ring. Henri has placed an ad in the *Casket* weekly. Trees, shrubs, flowers planted. Gardens prepared. Lawns raked. Will do anything. Which is true. Jobs are scarce around Antigonish.

Henri comes to Antigonish County by a different route than his friends. Unable to shake off a fascination with North America stemming from a high school exchange spent in Iowa, he returns to Holland, but soon finagles a job that brings him back-- this time to the farm of Joe Van Oirschot in Pleasant Valley, Nova Scotia. Bewitched by the wildness and beauty of rural Nova Scotia, Henri works on the farm, cuts pulpwood on the side, shoots a moose, fishes for trout, and buys the old farm across the valley.

The farm, including the house he is in today, belonged to John Joe Smith, who lived there all his life. Johnny Joe had grown too old to keep the place up and had decided to sell. In the 70's, many old timers sold their farms cheaply, or simply abandoned them. Young Nova Scotians were heading to the cities for good wages and had no interest in keeping up the family farm. So, for better or worse, they were there for the pickin'. The Farm Loan Board put up the money and Henri had the farm.

The phone rings.

Someone turns down the stereo. Conversation stops. Henri picks up the phone. *Hello? Yes, you need someone to build a fence? Yes, of course. You want it built of birch poles from the woods? Yes, we can do that. Your name and address? We'll be there first thing tomorrow. Thank you.* Henri hangs up. The room erupts in cheers. A job! And a business is born.

Duly registered with the Province in 1974, and christened Pleasant Valley Nurseries, Henri's enterprise, born that day in the old farmhouse, was to last 44 years despite fierce and unrelenting competition from box stores and large chains. The business, a ship sailed by Henri and his wife Phyllis and manned by a loyal crew of plant lovers, rose to become one of the best in Canada. A classic family-owned small-town business from start to finish, Pleasant Valley Nurseries owed its success primarily to increasingly sophisticated gardeners from across the Maritimes who sought its superb plant selection and knowledgeable staff. Towns, local businesses, and garden clubs provided valuable support.

The colourful and ever-changing variety of plants for sale attracted an equally colourful and ever-changing lineup of plant lovers hoping for work. Many came and went. Artists, musicians and students of all stripes were well represented, but usually moved on. Others, the born gardeners, joined to learn the ropes. Some worked for a period of time, then left to start businesses of their own. Several of us made a career of it. We built homes, raised our children, and can thank Henri and Phyllis Steeghs and Pleasant Valley Nurseries for a lifetime of friendship and gainful employment.

The little business was a success story of dedication, planning, and teamwork, and began as Henri's dream.

Henri dreaming...

Bruce Partridge

The dream

The dream was to grow and sell trees. This, Henri said, was the only thing that he really knew how to do. As a teenager in Holland he had worked in nurseries and learned to prune, graft and work with trees. Now (1970), in his early twenties and a recent immigrant to Canada, he thought this might be a good way to make a living.

It wasn't just the money, either. Henri really cared for trees. He wanted to provide trees to the good people of Antigonish County so they could beautify their properties and grow their own fruit. He wanted to be a useful citizen in this new country he had chosen.

Meanwhile, one way to make money was to work on a farm. Henri worked first for Joe van Oirschot and then for Casey van de Sande—both dairy farmers who had immigrated to Canada after World War II. They were amused by this young upstart from the old country and were eager to show him how things were done in Nova Scotia—like how to use the power saw and to wait next time until the season was open before shooting a moose. Henri took advice seriously and quickly adapted to life in rural Nova Scotia. In the summer he worked for the farmers and in the winter he cut pulpwood, and he saved his money.

Even as he worked on the farms and in the woods, Henri was growing trees and shrubs from cuttings and seeds he gathered as he travelled around. He had constructed a small shade house on the farm where he worked and was rooting cuttings inside, where they were protected from the hot sun. Outside, he prepared small seed beds in which to grow trees such as oak, maple, ash and birch. At this point, his plans to sell trees were rather vague, and he was growing them more or less for the fun of it.

The fun, though, was going to have to wait. That summer, 1972, Henri was at Casey's farm on the tractor when two men, Dick Morton and John Morley, drove up asking for him. It turns out that someone in Truro had learned somehow that Henri was interested in plants. John, who had just arrived from the Niagara Parks School of Horticulture in Niagara Falls, Ontario, was teaching a brand-new program of Ornamental Horticulture at the Nova Scotia Agricultural College and was rounding up students. He wanted Henri. Tuition was free and Henri didn't need much persuading. In the Fall he was off to Truro for his first year of Horticulture.

The Ornamental Horticulture program was heavy on landscape design and plant identification. Students learned to evaluate a property and draw landscape plans for it. The course also covered the science of plant growth, propagation, pruning, grafting and tree surgery, including how to climb with ropes and harness. In addition, the grounds at the Agriculture College featured rockeries and orchards, a small arboretum and turf trials where students learned about grass.

This was a two-year diploma program, and a revelation for those who wanted to learn how to garden and grow plants. Horticulture eh? So that's what you call it. The new program pulled in students from every corner of the compass, and taught them horticulture. If there was going to be a Pleasant Valley Nurseries, they would be ready. Henri was in the very first class and there was no 'Nurseries' yet. Finishing his year, though, he was convinced that this is what he would do in Antigonish.

While in Truro, he met Dick Morton again, and Les Blackburn, the provincial horticulturists for Nova Scotia. Dick and Les were more than encouraging and willing to help Henri with his dream. Once or twice the next summer they drove all the way to Pleasant Valley to check out Henri's setup and offer advice. They introduced him to Charlie Embree in Kentville, who was the provincial fruit tree specialist. Henri was particularly interested in grafting and producing fruit trees at his nursery. He thought that apple trees, especially, would sell well around Antigonish.

At this time, apple growers and producers were just beginning to adopt what were called "size-controlling" rootstocks for apple trees. Most of these were developed in Europe. Apple trees grafted onto size-controlling rootstocks were significantly smaller than old-fashioned apple trees, and earlier bearing. By choosing the right rootstock, you might produce an apple tree small enough to let you pick its fruit from the ground without a ladder. Obviously, this would appeal to a homeowner with a small property. The trouble was that these trees required better than average soil, which was rare in this part of Nova Scotia, and many were not hardy enough for our climate.

Henri says that Charlie Embree was the only one he talked to in Kentville who realized that conditions in this area were not the same as in the Annapolis valley. Charlie was able to recommend size-controlling rootstocks that would be successful here. Try Antonovka, Alnarp 2 and Malling Merton 111, he suggested. The only place they were growing these was in Oregon. Determined to try them in Pleasant Valley, Henri placed an order.

Charlie was a friend to Henri in other ways, taking him seriously and introducing him to scientists and researchers at the Kentville research station. Everyone at the research station was helpful and treated Henri with respect despite his youth and what some would consider his grandiose nursery plans. These professionals dealt with nurserymen and growers all across the Maritimes and didn't consider Henri's plans at all unrealistic. This was a great boost to Henri's confidence and the feeling that his ambitions were legitimate and had some weight behind them.

By 1974, Henri was finished with school. He had stocked his 12 acres in Pleasant Valley with young maples, birches and lindens, and the apple rootstocks were in the ground, awaiting grafting. He had enlarged his shade building for growing and propagating shrubs. His business was officially registered with the province—Pleasant Valley Nurseries.

At this point, says Henri, he figured that if he continued to grow a better and better selection of trees, fruit trees and shrubs, there would be somewhere to sell them. This "somewhere" was rather nebulous and Henri was still a long way from thinking of opening a retail garden centre. There wasn't much to sell yet, anyway, so he was back working on the farms and in the woods. The difference was that, with the expense of setting up a working nursery in Pleasant Valley, money was even tighter. He was, however, getting a reputation as a capable landscaper, and getting some work in that line. He didn't know it yet, but landscaping was going to help pay the bills for a long, long time to come.

The first big break was a job in Spring, 1975, planting an entire trailer court on Hawthorne Street for Hugh James Sullivan. There was a great deal of work and a valuable boost to the business. The planting required lots of topsoil—forty dump truck loads, to be exact.

Henri hired helpers from among the eager young hippies and back-to-the-landers around Antigonish. They put in lawns and planted trees from the nursery in Pleasant Valley. Besides the money, this job was important in other ways. Obviously, a job of this size was encouraging and a sign to Henri that he was on the right track. He was also coming to realize that he would need a dependable, steady outlet for the trees from his nursery. Maybe the first inkling of a future garden centre stirred in his head.

Henri was back at the nursery next summer in Pleasant Valley, with a larger shade-house and trees in the field, and, yes, a little garden centre. The inkling had borne fruit. He could now sell trees retail. He dug a pond and installed a pump for water. He built and painted attractive plywood signs advertising his new logo and the name of the business.

Now he found that operating a garden centre meant you had to stay around to talk to customers. No more working on landscape jobs in town. Money, consequently, was going out faster than it was coming in.

Henri will be embarrassed when he reads this, but he was, to a certain extent, the quintessential penniless immigrant. Sure, there was work around, but it didn't pay much, and there was certainly nothing left over to build a garden centre with. Henri was short of rich uncles. He needed a better selection of stock to tempt customers, and his nursery still needed work.

He had no choice but to go to the bank for a loan. The Bank of Nova Scotia agreed that a garden centre should do well in this area.

The loans manager, Frank Campbell, liked the idea so well that he not only approved Henri's loan but quit the bank to become his partner.

With a new business partner and money to spend, the Pleasant Valley Nurseries garden centre plan was taking shape. Over the winter Henri put together a typewritten planting guide and catalogue, listing the plants he had for sale. He placed ads in newspapers in Antigonish and neighbouring counties with a coupon to mail in for a free catalogue. He put up his brand-new plywood signs at the nursery and at the bottom of the Pleasant Valley Road to direct motorists from town. He hired a new man, Al Benoit, to help at the nursery. Al lived in Pomquet but had done horticulture school in Maine. He liked trees.

Business was sporadic that first summer. Few people found their way out the 7 km. of rough, often muddy, gravel road to Pleasant Valley. Those who did were a bit puzzled why someone would be selling trees and shrubs when the woods were full of them. Henri cheerfully showed them around the nursery—pointing out trees and shrubs they wouldn't find in the woods. Visitors arrived curious and left as customers, he hoped.

One day, Henri had a surprise visit from John Duykers who had driven out to Pleasant Valley with flats of colourful annual flowers in his trunk. John, whom Henri had not previously met, was building up a business growing and selling bedding plants from his greenhouses in Afton. He insisted that Henri keep the flowers and pay him for them only if they sold. Henri, dubious and somewhat unwilling to get involved selling annual flowers, reluctantly set them in the shade house with the nursery stock. To his "utter horror," as he puts it, John's flowers sold within the week. It was obvious what gardeners were looking for in those days.

John continued to bring out flowers that summer, and they continued to sell. As a matter of fact, Henri and John Duykers became good friends and John grew bedding plants for Pleasant Valley Nurseries for many years.

One visitor to Pleasant Valley that summer, Colin H. Chisholm, introduced himself as the owner of the Antigonish Mall. Henri was duly impressed to be in the company of someone who owned a mall. Mr. Chisholm came out several times that summer and obviously liked trees. Henri enjoyed his visits and learned eventually that Mall owner Chisholm was also the mayor of Antigonish. Mayor Chisholm's opinion, upon seeing Henri's little operation, was that he should set up in town. "Come look me up at the Mall sometime," he said. Henri made a note of that.

That Fall, PVN was looking to increase their supply and selection of trees and shrubs. Henri placed an order with Sheridan Nurseries in Ontario. The idea was that if he ordered in the Fall and wintered the plants over himself, he would save money. The order would come on the train, which still served Antigonish in those days. The railway maintained a station and freight sheds along the tracks.

Also, Henri had struck a deal with a retiring nurseryman to buy his remaining stock. This stock, however, would not come on the train. It was all growing in the ground and would require a digging expedition to the Annapolis Valley. Both the order from Ontario and the digging trip to the Valley were to have repercussions.

Henri says that the digging trip, with his friend and co-worker Derf Chisholm, was pivotal for Pleasant Valley Nurseries. It started badly. It was Sunday—the seventh day—the only day Henri could get away after working the other six. The work was going to be hard and slow and it was a long drive to the Valley. Henri wanted to start early. Digging trees requires two men, and Derf had agreed to go with him.

The trouble was that Derf had gone to a dance in Larry's River on Saturday night and now, Sunday morning, was still there. Remember, these boys were only in their twenties. The upshot was that Henri had to drive to Larry's River—fifty kilometres in the wrong direction—to pick Derf up. Finally on their way, a little bit late, twenty kilometres west of Antigonish in Marshy Hope, they had a flat tire. No spare. On this moment hung the fate of Pleasant Valley Nurseries. Worn out, discouraged, deep in debt and suspecting that the entire enterprise was flawed, Henri nearly quit.

The boys, however, were able to get the wheel off the truck and roll it to a repair shop which was, miraculously, not far away. Once they got the tire fixed, Henri and Derf and Pleasant Valley Nurseries continued on.

The truck returned with a load of plants from the Valley, which the team tucked into pots and planting beds in Pleasant Valley. Later, the order from Ontario arrived as scheduled. Henri made sure that these plants were safe in the shade house with their roots buried in loose sawdust. The shade house itself was sealed up for the winter with a cover of white plastic to moderate extremes of temperature. There was no reason why plants should not be in perfect shape for Spring.

Through the winter, Henri worked on the new catalogue. From time to time he checked on the plants in the shade house and watered them if they were too dry. Everything looked good. This winter Henri and his partner Frank also signed up for a conference on treatment strategies for Dutch Elm disease. The conference was to be in Ottawa in March and would bring together experts from across the continent. Henri and Frank hoped to learn how they might establish a program to save the majestic elms of Antigonish county. The government was expected to provide grants for initiatives of this kind, so there might be support money to get it going. In the meantime, Henri remembered to look up Mayor Chisholm at the Mall. True to his word, the mayor thought he could help Pleasant Valley Nurseries set up in town come Spring.

In March, Henri and Frank went up to attend the course in Ottawa. Henri remembers that it was put on by an agency of the federal government and fifty or sixty tree professionals from across Canada and the USA attended. They were there to study and discuss control of the Dutch elm disease which had devastated elms throughout the US northeast and central states and into Canada. It was just appearing in the Maritimes and looked as if it could still be stopped. An Asian fungus spread by an elm beetle caused the disease, and it had already cut a swath through Europe. The fungus had been identified and isolated by a couple of Dutch scientists—hence "Dutch" elm disease. The disease epidemic in North America, though, probably started from a shipment of contaminated elm logs from France.

At the course, arborists learned that the strategy to stop elm disease was threefold. First, the bark beetles that spread the disease might be eradicated by spraying insecticide into the treetops with high-pressure sprayers. Second, the fungus itself might be killed by fungicides injected into the sap of the tree at its base. Third, diseased trees must be taken down and burned before the infection could spread to healthy trees. This was termed "sanitation".

Not one of these three strategies was simple, and not one was effective by itself. The biggest obstacle was the enormous size of the tree. Even the highest-powered sprayers couldn't reach into the tops of the trees to do a good job. The trees were so massive at the base that injected fungicides really couldn't spread through the sap of the entire tree, and the immense size of the elm made removal and burning of infected trees a daunting, dangerous and expensive proposition. Henri and Frank left the conference optimistic, nevertheless, that Nova Scotia could save its elms.

Henri, back home in Antigonish, met with officials and delivered a presentation to the public, hoping to get a sanitation program started to save the local elms. This might have meant a government grant and maybe a job, but the reality was that small towns in Nova Scotia, for the most part, couldn't come up with the kind of money an effective program would require, so the town lost its elms, and there was no work for Henri.

There was, however, an interesting proposition from the Mayor. He was ready to offer space in the parking lot of the Mall to set up a garden sales area for Spring of 1977. There was an A-frame shed alongside the entrance next to the A&W restaurant that was there in those days. The shed was vacant and Henri could use it. There would be lots of traffic, Mayor Chisholm assured him.

Both Henri and Frank thought it was worth a try despite challenges such as arranging fencing and water supply. There was much to do to get ready. And there was a cruel lesson waiting for Henri back at the nursery.

It was the beautiful shipment of plants that Henri had received from Sheridans back in the Fall. Checking on them in the shade house as he had done regularly during the winter, his heart fell to his stomach. Mice. Something he had failed to anticipate. Almost every plant was girdled. Mice had gnawed the bark from around the base of nearly every one. These were probably doomed, and certainly unsaleable. Henri knew that rabbits and deer could ruin trees, and he took measures to prevent this, but mice he had ignored—something he would never do again.

He would have to scramble to gather enough plants to sell at the Mall, and the bank wasn't going to be happy. Once again he wondered if it was all worth it.

Bruce Partridge

The move to town

The move to the Mall soon dispelled Henri's doubts. In fact, he says it was a monumental step forward for Pleasant Valley Nurseries. Mayor Chisholm's offer was brilliant. PVN was moving on, with the disaster with the mice only a bitter lesson.

Henri and Frank set up a temporary fenced enclosure at the Mall with the little A-frame for an office and stocked it with plants from Pleasant Valley. Some of the Sheridan's order was okay. They had oaks, maples, birch, ash and red maple—some started from seed and some dug from the woods. That was permissible then. They also had a few trees from John Westenenk's nursery in Marydale, and shrubs started from cuttings.

Just as Mayor Chisholm had promised, traffic was steady past their little enterprise. They were only set up at the Mall for a few weeks, but were amazed at the number of people pulling in to look and ask questions. Some of them even bought trees.

Few people in Antigonish had ever seen a proper garden centre. Fancy trees and shrubs might be obtained from Sears, which ordered them from the McConnell nurseries in Ontario. By the time plants made it from McConnell's, through the Sears network, to the outlet in Antigonish, though, they were likely to be in pretty rough shape. Pruned to fit in a box, dried up and leafless, they certainly didn't look like the picture in the catalogue.

Building supplies and hardware stores sold some plants early in the season. but didn't know what they had or how to take care of them. People were very excited to see living trees and shrubs for sale, complete with leaves and flowers. In three weeks, Henri says, they made more sales than they had in a whole summer in Pleasant Valley.

After the success at the Mall, the guys were determined to build a real garden centre in town. Henri began to look for land. His sometime employer and mentor, Casey van de Sande, offered a piece at the end of Hawthorne Street, but it wasn't ideal.

At the office of deeds and records was a map of all the holdings in Antigonish with names neatly written in ink. Casey's lot was at one end of the map. At the other end, Henri noticed, was a property with the owner's name written in pencil—a brand new acquisition. The name was Willie Westenenk, and the property looked like it just might be right for a garden centre.

Henri was well acquainted with John Westenenk but had never met Willie, who was John's brother. He did know, however, that Willie supervised the grounds at St. Francis Xavier University and knew a thing or two about plants.

One day at the Post Office, Henri spotted a man who he was sure must be Willie. Sure enough, it was. Gathering up his courage, Henri approached and introduced himself. Ramping up his courage even further, Henri inquired if he might buy a piece of Willie's land for a nursery. Finally, going for broke, he asked Willie if he might pay for this land over time since he had no money.

The rest is history. Willie agreed on all counts. He was eager to provide land for a nursery and was generous enough to work out long-term financing. Willie has been our neighbour at Pleasant Valley Nurseries and an honorary member of the staff ever since.

By the Fall of 1977, arrangements concluded, Henri got ready to build.

The building foundation in fashion among do-it-yourselfers in that era was used railroad ties stood on end. An eight-foot tie cut in two gave two posts. You bury a post three feet into the ground and enough sticks up to build on. No one was sure how long these posts would last before rotting, but estimates ranged from ten to twenty years. This seemed long enough to one who was twenty years old himself. Henri couldn't have dreamed that his building would still be standing forty years later.

Before freeze-up that Fall, Henri and Frank had posts in the ground and were ready to build the garden store—20 by 20. The design of the building was an original, drawn out by Henri "on the back of a napkin" and determined by "the length of the lumber and the size of the nails."

Building codes were non-existent in 1977—at least Henri didn't know of any. Some remarkable structures were built in those days by folks building for themselves with no money, no experience and no fear. Building alone, for the most part, through the winter, with hand tools and the chainsaw, Henri got the store done, although there was no electrical power yet.

Built with rough lumber, used windows and doors, and staggered cedar shingles, the building was unique. It was low and cute and perfect for a garden centre. Enthroned inside this fairy-tale building, besides a counter and shelves, was an enormous cash register retired from the liquor store, ready to be filled. It looked like it might have come from a San Francisco brothel. Covered with golden scrolls and curlicues, it had keys like an old-fashioned typewriter and must have weighed two hundred pounds. Inside were thousands of tiny springs, gears and cogs that spun and whirred. Though in a power outage this miraculous contraption could be operated with a crank, it was modern enough that it could be plugged in.

Bruce Partridge

Donald MacLellan of the Antigonish Electrical Utility had promised that if Henri got his store built, he would hook up the power. To his surprise, but not Henri's, the store did get built, so Donald dutifully connected the power. The cash register sprang to life. It wasn't too long before the town crew hooked up water, and the store was ready to stock with fertilizer and supplies.

Around this time, Henri joined the Atlantic Provinces Nursery Trades Association. Dick Morton and Les Blackburn, the provincial horticulturists, promoted the APTNA to unite everyone doing business in landscaping or horticulture in the region to share experiences and resources. Dick and Les were working with the new horticulture program at the Nova Scotia Agriculture College in Truro and wanted to see a wider and more ambitious variety of ornamental plants and plantings in the Maritimes. Henri says that these were the first men he had met who were genuinely interested in new plant introductions, their hardiness and suitability to this area, and their use in the landscape. This was a great help for Henri and others planning to go into business for themselves.

A respectable number of nursery operators and landscapers across the Maritimes embraced the APNTA. Each year, in the middle of winter, there was a general business meeting featuring speakers and presentations, to which everyone was invited. The meeting began with a rundown of the finances and concerns of the organization and of the members—a business meeting, in other words—chaired by whoever was president that year. Then came the speakers and presentations, and then the best part, the open bar. The Association in those years was very generous with the liquor and in no time at all everyone was relaxed, laughing, sharing stories with fellow "landscrapers", and picking up advice from the old fellows. The annual meeting took place in a different city each year. I remember meetings in Truro and Moncton, and there must have been at least one in Halifax. Each meeting chose new officers for the next year.

One year, Henri was chosen to be president. The meeting that winter would be in Moncton. Henri and Phyllis were going, of course, and a few of us from Pleasant Valley Nurseries were going with them. A day or two before the meeting was to take place, Henri was working feverishly, as usual, trying to get some last moment plumbing done at the garden centre. He had parked his truck by the front door. In the back of the truck was a long piece of ¾ inch copper pipe, tipped up over the tailgate and butted up solidly against the back of the cab. At the speed Henri was working, it was inevitable. Striding straight toward the back of the truck, he had forgotten the pipe sticking out. It took him between the eyes, knocking him to his knees, and leaving him with a bloody ¾-inch circle exactly in the centre of his forehead.

The day of the meeting arrived and Henri was president. We all drove to Moncton. Chairing the meeting, Henri was dressed nattily in slacks and a blazer, and maybe a tie—I can't remember—but in the centre of his forehead was that circle, scabbed over and fiery red. Now, most of the members of the APNTA were older gentlemen, and they were a bit skeptical of Henri anyway, with his beard and longish hair. That circle must have looked to them like the bloody brand of some Satanic cult. They were gentlemen, though, and held their tongues.

Henri acquitted himself well and the meeting was a success. We adjourned to the free bar where, to everyone's relief and amusement, the whole story came out. Those hard-bitten old nurserymen and landscapers knew what it was like to hurt yourself, and between the sympathy and the liquor, Henri was firmly in their good books.

Over the years, many became his friends and mentors. Bob Bezzant, an older Brit who had built a solid nursery business—Spruce Lane—in New Brunswick, took Henri under his wing. Jim, Peggy, and Ross Godfrey of Atlantic Gardens became friends and he connected with Bob Osborn—a man of about his own age—who was starting up Corn Hill Nurseries near Sussex, and shared many of the same challenges. Warren Tregunno of Halifax Seed became a key confidant and mentor. Henri did more and more business with Halifax Seed as years went on and had great respect for Warren, and later his son Tim, who he says were both real gentlemen.

With the store just about finished, the business needed a greenhouse in which to keep tender flowers and garden transplants. Henri's nurseryman friend in Marydale, John Westenenk, donated some homemade wooden greenhouse arches that he was no longer using. The boys put them up and covered them with plastic. The new little greenhouse looked very smart attached to the store and filled with flowers from John Duykers.

Opposite the greenhouse, on the other side of the store, Henri and Frank put up a little lath house. This lath house, or shade house, was a framework covered with wooden strips to provide shade for plants that need it. On a hot summer day, it could be very nice in the filtered sun and humidity of the lath house.

With the store built and stocked, the little greenhouse and the lath house up, trees and shrubs in the yard, and a young woman from B.C., Phyllis Baker, at the fancy cash register, Pleasant Valley Nurseries was ready for customers. Henri says he had thought of everything except the mud.

Ready to go!

The new Pleasant Valley Nurseries was built in what was formerly a cow pasture. The soil was heavy clay covered with grass. With the Spring rains coming down, and frost out of the ground, cars going in and out of the garden centre soon broke through the sod, and the mud was phenomenal. Cars could get in but they got stuck trying to leave. It sounds comical now, but it wasn't. It was embarrassing and bad for business. Henri owned an old 4-wheel drive Land Rover with a broken starter motor. He used it to tow out one customer after another and left it running so he didn't have to start it with the crank. This situation was impossible and Henri went looking to buy gravel to cover the mud.

He was lucky that he went to Finley Brophy—a trucker he knew slightly from Pleasant Valley. Henri was asking for one load of gravel, which in retrospect, was ridiculous. Finley brought nine. Furthermore, he wouldn't take money right away. To this day, Henri isn't sure he ever paid for that gravel, though Finley assures him that he did. He'll always be grateful to Finley for bailing him out.

Justifiably proud of the spanking new garden centre they had built, Henri and Frank had to figure out how to make it pay. Henri was ramping up production at the nursery and had designed and printed an attractive catalogue of "hardy plants for Northeastern Nova Scotia". He was bringing in an expanded selection of exotic—for Antigonish—trees and shrubs, and trusted that this would entice the customers.

The inescapable reality, however, was that Pleasant Valley Nurseries was, and always would be, a small, seasonal business in a small town. The largest portion by far of income from the store came in two months—May and June. After that, people had their gardens planted, customers were scarce to non-existent, and it was only money going out.

Considering this, Frank figured that along with the store and nursery, they should field a crew doing landscaping and landscape maintenance to bring in steady money and help take up the slack. They would be hiring men to work in town and at the nursery through the busy months of May and June anyway, and it felt wrong to simply let them go after that. If Pleasant Valley Nurseries could drum up maintenance contracts and landscaping work, the men could be bringing in money through the quiet months, he reasoned.

By Spring, the catalogue of "hardy plants for Northern Nova Scotia" was out and in the hands of customers. Henri left stacks with the post office to leave in mail boxes. He placed ads in newspapers including a coupon to send in for a catalogue. I had just been hired on and we were all passing them out at the store at every opportunity. In addition, by Summer, there was a landscaping crew.

The landscaping years

Landscaping happened. It began with a letter from the Michelin Tire Company in New Glasgow asking if PVN would be interested in taking over the mowing and lawn maintenance at the plant and around the houses they owned in Stellarton. Henri and Frank couldn't help feeling flattered that big companies were already taking them seriously. Frank was especially pleased and a contract was signed with Michelin.

PVN bought mowers, and worked out contracts with the CJFX radio station and the R.K. MacDonald nursing home, which both had large areas of lawn. We hired more workers, and lured Bruce Davidson away from the Met store in the mall to work with Al Benoit on yard work and planting.

I was to do the mowing along with Pete Stovell, a popular local blues musician who had done lawn maintenance in Ontario. It was ironic that I was mowing the lawns at the Michelin tire plant, because a year before I had been working there making tires. Now, as I was mowing, I could see my old crew mates out on the step taking their break and staring in amazement, wondering how I got out.

Money from these mowing contracts was welcome, and requests were coming in for planting work from homeowners and businesses that didn't want to attempt it themselves. Henri was still apprehensive about sending men and trucks out onto the road day after day, fearing that tired landscapers might fall asleep at the wheel. We were lucky that nothing like this ever happened.

Planting and landscaping became an integral part of business at Pleasant Valley Nurseries for almost the next thirty years, featuring a revolving cast of characters, and the stories are legendary. Having our own truck and equipment and a trained crew was the answer for the many customers who bought plants but needed someone to plant them. Owners of businesses and newly built homes often needed fairly extensive plantings. This allowed us to sell plants as well as providing work for three or four rough-and-tumble landscapers in a truck.

Mary and Henri supervise economy studs.

The landscapers were also handy to have around the garden centre if there happened to be yard work going on. We were an essential work force for the myriad of dirty jobs around the place. These included planting and digging up trees and shrubs in the field, helping to construct new buildings, covering greenhouses, fencing, digging post holes and drainage ditches of every description, loading and unloading trucks, and now and then taking the garbage to the dump.

This was before Vernon Dee started the Eastern Sanitation Ltd. company and before we got the beautiful big blue steel garbage box. We tossed all the garbage we generated in a pile behind the greenhouse until it went to the dump. Since the landscape crew was supposed to be out landscaping and making money, and there was no money in hauling garbage, it didn't get picked up very often.

The time I am going to tell you about, we had been doing a lot of building and renovating around the place, as well as our ordinary work with the plants. The garbage pile had grown to unprecedented proportions. All the construction debris was on the pile. This included lumber with nails, rain-soaked pink insulation, decomposing gyprock, plastic pipe, wire and tin. On the pile as well were a large quantity of worn-out plant pots, broken bamboo stakes, dirty sheets of plastic and Styrofoam from the greenhouse, and dozens of wet, soggy broken-down cardboard boxes. This was long before cardboard could be recycled. The whole pile was well soaked and settled in the rain, and it smelled.

One day, the word went out to take the garbage to the dump no matter if there was landscaping going on or not. We backed the landscaping truck—a ton truck with a large box and five-foot sides—up to the pile and started loading the mess. The pile was huge but we were determined to take it all in one load. There was no way we wanted to have to drive to the dump twice in one day.

Incredibly, we did it. Garbage stuck up over the box but we threw a net over it. Then the back doors wouldn't close. Almost but not quite. Accustomed to problems like this on landscaping jobs, we simply fished a broken-up piece of plywood out of the load, shut the doors as far as they would go, and nailed the plywood across them to hold them closed. There. Done.

Pretty proud of ourselves for getting all the garbage on in one load, we took off for Brierly Brook, which was where the dump was then. Arriving at the dump, we got out to unload.

The first sign of trouble was that the plywood was gone and the doors were swinging open. Also, there was a lot less garbage on the truck than we had left with. That's when our friend Regan MacGillivray slid to a stop behind us to inform us that the Brierly Brook road was covered in garbage all the way from town. He was on his way to the dump right behind us and said he had to drive like Mario Andretti to get around it all. Ten minutes later, it was Henri Steeghs who arrived to tell us that irate homeowners on the

Bruce Partridge

Brierly Brook road were ringing the phone off the hook at PVN and threatening legal action if the mess was not cleaned up totally, and right away. With our company name painted proudly on the side of the truck, there was no question of who was the guilty party.

So, after unloading what garbage remained on the truck, we drove slowly back to town-- one man driving and two men on the running boards—picking filthy garbage from the road and the ditches and tossing it back onto the truck, arriving back at the garden centre with almost as much garbage as we had started out with.

We did a good job picking up and drove it all back to the dump, but it took all day and still it was weeks before the squabble died down. Badly chastened, the three of us were relieved to get back to the relatively routine business of landscaping.

Frank Campbell took care of accounts at PVN, and also led the landscape crew on jobs the first Summer. By the next, he had chosen to take a position as manager of the Antigonish arena. From this time on, Henri's soon-to-be partner and wife, Phyllis Baker, looked after ordering, payroll, and accounts.

We didn't know it then, but Phyllis was going to keep this shaky new business together. She had a talent for dealing with suppliers and balancing accounts and wasn't likely to quit. Unlike Henri and I, she was able to look at the business realistically and determine what was actually profitable. On top of that, she was a walking encyclopedia of plants and a formidable green thumb. Henri told me many times—and I know he is sincere—that without Phyllis, PVN would never have made it.

Dave Hoar was the first full-time landscape foreman PVN hired to replace Frank. Dave was a wiry little hockey player from Moncton, a likeable guy and a graduate of the Ornamental Horticulture program at the Agricultural College in Truro. He divided his time between drawing landscape plans for customers and working with the crew.

Dave and Henri worked out and adopted the raised planting bed, which became our style from then on. The raised bed improved the look of a planting immensely, and lifted plants up out of the cold clay. In the loose, warm and fertile soil of the raised bed, there was no stopping them. We mulched them with bark chips to keep down weeds and retain moisture, and we had a winning combination.

Dave Hoar.

By this time, along with planting, the landscapers had a lot of work looking after plantings—fertilizing, pruning and mulching, and Dave had to schedule all this work in, too. Henri always claimed that Dave, who had some uncommon religious beliefs, had super powers. I guess Dave got tired of us asking him to levitate the peat moss, because he took off to Israel to look after gardens there.

Over the winter it sank in. Dave Hoar had been doing all the landscape plans and leading the landscaping crew. I'm afraid we took him for granted. Spring of 1983 was looming, and we were going to have to find a replacement fast. I couldn't do it. My job was keeping the garden centre shipshape. Henri was out of the question.

Bruce Partridge

Around the last of March, Henri and I were in the greenhouse where it was warm, looking forlornly at the mess we were going to have to tackle soon and wondering how we were ever going to replace Dave. Snowbanks were still high outside and the only trail to the greenhouse was a long one through knee-deep snow. We didn't expect to be disturbed, but we were.

Stepping high through the snowbanks into the greenhouse and stamping the snow off her boots, came my future wife—Mary MacLean from Long Point, Cape Breton. More importantly, she could draw landscape plans. She was another graduate of the Horticulture program at the NSAC and had been working in Halifax at Mt. St. Vincent University. We took a look at a couple of plans she had drawn and she had the job.

Jack MacLeod

Now we needed a landscape foreman and we got one—Jack MacLeod. Jack was a rather unlikely landscaper—a freewheeling motorcyclist who had been employed as a master printer at the *Casket* newspaper printing shop. Jack insisted, though, that he wanted to work with plants, and was so convincing and persistent that Henri hired him on. This was no mistake as Jack was a hard worker and as good as his word. He learned his plants and picked up the planting and the plant maintenance business quickly.

The planting crew usually included Jack, myself, Paul Chisholm and Bruce Davidson. Paul—from Heatherton—was an accomplished gardener and a graduate of the Agriculture College. He was a valuable worker when he wasn't trying to cut his head off with the power saw. Ask him about the scars on his chest!

Bruce Davidson deserves special mention. He was one of the first men Henri hired when he discovered Bruce working unhappily at the Met. Bruce was from Tidnish Bridge near Amherst. He had no desire to lead the crew but worked with us on virtually every job we ever did. There was no one at PVN who sparked as much controversy as he did. He was an endless source of entertainment and exasperation—a gossip and a tease and a gifted bullshitter. Nevertheless, we all loved him, especially the girls. Sadly, he passed away a few years ago in Tidnish, far too young.

Doug Myer, Chris Griffiths, and Bill Briand ("Willie Hop") worked with us. Doug went on to manage the grounds at St.F.X. University, afterwards starting a planting business of his own, as did Bill. Chris became the Antigonish town gardener. Besides us old timers, we usually had a summer student in the truck, or one of Henri's sons—cocky high school boys whom Doug Myer called the economy studs. The economy studs often didn't stay for more than a year or two, and had no interest in horticulture, but Henri and I figured we offered a valuable service: turning boys into men and showing them why they should stay in school.

It wasn't unusual to bring Mary along on planting jobs since she had drawn the plan, and by mid-summer when plant sales slowed down, other women from the garden centre often pitched in. Linda Petite and Janette Fecteau, and especially Holly Chisholm, Paul's wife, put in time and showed that landscaping was not just a man's game.

Bruce Partridge

The style and methods of planting introduced by PVN—groupings of plants in raised beds with bark mulch—were effective, admired, and widely copied, fundamentally changing the look of landscaping in this end of Nova Scotia. Over the years, Henri and Phyllis at the Pleasant Valley Nurseries garden centre introduced hundreds of new varieties of trees, shrubs and perennials which were worked into landscape designs and planted by the crew. Plants such as rhododendrons, magnolias, Japanese maples and many others—once considered hopelessly exotic—are now widely planted and enrich the local landscape. Subtract the landscaping work done or inspired by Pleasant Valley Nurseries over the last forty years, and the Antigonish area would be a different place indeed.

Over these years, PVN earned a reputation for conscientious planting work and tasteful landscape design. Up until the year 2000, while Pleasant Valley Nurseries still had a landscaping crew, our landscape planning service was a key part of the business. Those of us doing the planning were graduates of that Ornamental Horticulture program at the Agricultural College (AC) in Truro, where planning and design were a big part of the curriculum. Dave Hoar, myself, my wife Mary and Henri all drew landscape plans at various times. A landscape plan from Pleasant Valley Nurseries involved a visit to the client's property where we took measurements and talked plants. For a modest fee, compared to that of a landscape architect, we would design a layout from the measurements we had taken, and suggest plantings that would be colourful and appropriate for the property. We drew the plan by hand to scale on a large sheet of drafting paper, just like we had been taught at the AC. These large, formal plans, treating the entire property, were in demand and we also did walk-in plans of small areas for free. Linda, Beverly, Holly, and Phyllis did a lot of these.

Using the plan, and spacing plants according to the scale of the drawing, clients could do their own planting if they chose. If they wanted an estimate for us doing the work, that was easy. We could add up the plants on the plan, estimate the time and materials, and come up with a price. If the planting took place, the crew knew just where and how big to make the beds, and how to arrange the plants. We were able to include plants on these plans which were quite unknown and unfamiliar in this area. This was fun for us and certainly enriched the "plantscape" of Antigonish County.

For many years the landscape plan was a cornerstone of the business and stimulated plant sales, kept the crew working, and brought in much needed revenue at times when sales were slow at the store. It introduced us to many enthusiastic homeowners and gardeners, and them to us. Landscape planning was a service quite unavailable anywhere else in this area and another feather in the cap for Pleasant Valley Nurseries.

Loading up.

A typical day of landscaping began early. With the plan in the truck, we would back up to the large pile of bark mulch at the bottom of the yard and fork on as much as we thought we would need, and then half as much again. What we thought we would need was never enough. We didn't want to be caught at the end of the day stretching bark, which was what we called it when we were running out and had to skimp to cover all the beds.

And we actually did fork it on the truck by hand, with hay forks. Often we needed at least half a truckload for the job, and the back of that ton truck with five foot sides sure looked big starting out in the morning. At that time the business had no tractor or other loader, but eventually we started keeping our bark at Kell's yard by the dairy and having them fill the truck with their loader.

After the bark, we loaded the rototiller and the sod cutter; then the peat moss, manure, fertilizer and limestone, and any concrete pavers or wooden timbers we would need. Finally, on went the plants. We knew just what plants we needed because we had the plan.

We had to pack the plants carefully, laying them down and covering them to protect them from being beaten up by the wind. We had a heavy net which worked better than plastic or a tarp, and sometimes we just covered them with bark mulch and dug them out upon arrival. We stuck the wheelbarrows, shovels, rakes, and other hand tools we needed into nooks and crannies in the load, or tied them on top.

Loaded last were the three or four landscapers, their spare boots and clothing, their gloves, their thermos and their lunch, all jammed into the cab of the truck, leaving barely enough elbow room for four cups of coffee for the road. We recovered from loading on the drive, which often took us through spectacular scenery to lovely properties we hadn't seen before.

At the job, we quickly unloaded everything but the bark mulch. We began by outlining the planting beds according to the plan, and removing the sod with the sod cutter. With our trusty Troy-bilt tiller we bounced over the newly exposed soil in the beds, trying to work in peat moss, manure, fertilizer and limestone, and bust them up a little. In this land of shale and clay, packed hard by construction equipment, we were happy if we got down five or six inches.

We knew from bitter experience that this was not enough, and we had learned to build up the beds with topsoil from a pile we had arranged ahead of time. We did this with shovel and wheelbarrow, piling the soil higher where the bed was wide and lower where it was narrow. This made for a planting with interesting contours.

When the topsoil was all in place, we spread the peat moss and other soil amendments we had saved for this stage, and rototilled it again. This time the soil was deep and loose and tilled up easily. We raked the beds back up and put in the plants, which was the easy part. At this point the total soil depth was a foot or so in the low spots, up to almost two feet where it was deep—plenty of fertile ground for trees and shrubs to get started in.

Finally, we shovelled bark off the truck straight into the wheelbarrows and covered the planting beds, hoping we wouldn't have to stretch the mulch this time. When everything was cleaned up, the work looked good, the plants perched up jauntily in the raised beds just where the plan said they should be—colourful against the dark mulch.

By now the shadows were getting long. The owners of the house and their neighbours were home and out on their decks admiring our work. As we cleaned up we could smell the barbecue and hear the ice cubes clinking in the glasses. Time to get home.

The years of landscaping became, unexpectedly, a priceless learning experience for the entire PVN staff. The crew was always on the road, planting almost anywhere in Pictou, Antigonish, or Guysborough counties, or Cape Breton. We were enthusiastic plant people and the travel and landscaping work was a god-sent opportunity to observe mature ornamental plantings and native plant communities and see what grew where.

We also got to know all too well the wide variety of challenging soil and growing conditions to be found in northeastern Nova Scotia and began to work out ways to deal with them. Landscape plantings were a valuable laboratory in which we could plant uncommon or unfamiliar plants that we wished to sell at the garden centre and see how they performed in this area. Some we only dared to try at home—hence the occasional dead or moribund Katsura or coffee tree, flowering cherry, apricot, almond, mulberry or the like to be glimpsed at our places.

Other trials, though, proved successful and we could introduce new species and varieties at our garden centre.. Years later. when landscaping was finished at Pleasant Valley Nurseries, we still drew on the experience and expertise we had gained in those years in order to help gardeners. It is what set us apart from the high-school kids selling plants at the big chain stores, and helped us survive.

Enthusiastic response to the landscape planning and planting services we offered meant we were travelling and planting steadily. Of the hundreds of planting jobs we completed over the years a few are particularly memorable. Among the most memorable were the first ones.

Fixing up Port Hawkesbury.

For Spring 1979, PVN had lined up a job laying sod on the steep banks around the new liquor store in Guysborough, and also had a contract to plant trees along some of the streets in Port Hawkesbury. We did the trees first. With the garden centre set up and ready to go, but before it got busy or the grass started to grow, we loaded the big truck—a three ton once used by the dairy—with trees and supplies, and Frank, who was at that time still our leader, took us to Port Hawkesbury.

Pampered by mowing lawns the year before with Pete Stovell, this was the first time I had been out of Antigonish to do work with the crew. It was my first encounter with Frank Campbell's policy that when you drove all the way to Port Hawkesbury to work, you didn't return home until the work was finished. Policy also said that you would finish this work no matter what the weather was doing. By 9 o'clock that night, working by the headlights of the truck, in the cold rain, with a splitting headache, putting the last of the trees in rock-hard soil, I was seriously questioning my career choice.

After that, it was easy to stay busy at the garden centre with Phyllis and Frank, and Henri when he wasn't in Pleasant Valley at the nursery. I was learning to sell plants and look after them. Doug Myer was mowing grass with Pete. Bruce Davidson and Al Benoit took care of any planting or tree maintenance around town, and there was no more landscaping with Frank until July, after business had calmed down at the garden centre and grass wasn't growing so fast. Then we did the Guysborough liquor store.

This job involved laying sods on banks behind the brand-new store. The banks were nearly vertical, and sods had to be laid on chicken wire and pegged so they didn't slide off. We had a couple of guys cutting sod at George Baxter's sheep farm in West River and running it to Guysborough, complete with sheep manure and thistles. There the rest of us were pegging it to a bank so steep that we were practically standing on each other's shoulders. I was beginning to learn that if a job was easy, people did it themselves. If it was nasty, they called us.

The sod cutter we used to cut the sod at George Baxter's farm is a story in itself. Before I ever saw it, I imagined a sod cutter to be like a tractor that would cut rolls of sod all ready to be loaded on the truck. What it turned out to be was a 400-pound beast with two handlebars, about the size of a rototiller. It was driven by a big, single-cylinder engine with no muffler. With that motor blasting and the sod-cutting blade shaking your teeth out, you pushed the thing through the soil and rocks with brute force—sometimes three men pushing and pulling at once. We used that machine for decades to remove the sods on landscaping jobs. Once it even fell off the back of the truck, but was okay. If it had a clean spark plug, you couldn't kill it. It's the reason I'm deaf today.

Henri himself had been trained at the Agricultural College to design landscapes. He was drawing occasional plans and lining up planting work. Before Dave Hoar's time, whenever Henri wasn't too busy at the garden centre or the nursery he took us out to do some of these jobs. At one house we did, I watched Henri plant three pyramid cedars in a triangle around the corner of the house, as on the plan he had drawn. I was impressed. This seemed impossibly bold and creative for those days when planting one pyramid cedar was a big deal. We laugh about it now because our landscape designs became much more imaginative as demand grew, but at that time it was courageous.

Another planting that Henri designed and took us to do was the Dairy Queen in Port Hawkesbury. Henri had big boulders trucked in and placed in spots where we would plant trees and shrubs around them. In between the boulders two big loads of topsoil had been dumped and waited to be spread for planting.

Getting out of the truck, I waited to see what sort of machine would arrive to do this spreading. To my amazement, Henri picked up two shovels, handed me one, and began to fill a wheelbarrow from the first pile. Evidently, we were going to move all that soil ourselves. Well, we did, and in much shorter order than I expected. Once the soil was in place, and fortified with peat moss and manure, we planted pines and junipers around the boulders—evergreens were in fashion then—and the finished effect was very impressive.

The reason I remember this job so clearly is that it taught me how much work a man with only a shovel and a wheelbarrow can do in a day. Later on, when we did hire backhoes, excavators and trucks, we often spent a great deal of time after they left fixing up ruts and torn sod and trees that had been skinned while "saving" us labour.

Trucks were in order, though, a few years later when we did an extensive planting of trees and shrubs below the Antigonish arena on James Street. This was on a rather steep bank that had been covered in grass for years. The soil—what there was of it—was thin, compacted, and worn out. We knew from experience that trees planted on this slope would have a hard time of it. The ground desperately needed organic matter to bulk up and rejuvenate the soil.

Our usual procedure was to rototill in bags of peat moss and manure from the garden centre. On a bank this size, though, the amounts of peat moss and dinky little bags of manure required were impossible. Undaunted, we pulled out the stops and ordered truck-loads of steaming cow manure straight from the farm. We worked tons of it into the soil, and were proud of the way those trees grew. Even Frank Campbell, who now worked at the arena, was impressed when he came out to tease us.

Of course, we had only proven again that there is nothing like honest-to-goodness farm manure to make things grow. What was true in gardening a thousand years ago is still true today.

Around this same time, we had the opportunity to do plantings at the new McDonald's restaurant that was opening in Antigonish. The proprietors, David Miller and his wife Aida Arnold, wanted a landscaping plan drawn up and were asking for plantings on a scale that was unheard of around fast food restaurants in those days. Aida, especially, was adamant that the planting be tasteful and, above all, colourful. She was well ahead of her time requesting that large numbers of perennial plants and bulbs be included in the planting to complement the shrubs.

Our landscape planner, Mary MacLean (not quite yet Partridge), was happy to comply. Her design featured a framework of small shrubs and trees, and, as instructed, beds of colourful perennials and groupings of spring-blooming bulbs. There was a push on to have the landscaping finished quickly so the restaurant could open. It kept everyone at Pleasant Valley Nurseries busy to get it finished. We planted a wide variety of plants, and were excited to see how they would fare in years to come. When the plants were in and mulched with bark mulch, it looked good right away.

Garth Lowther at McDonald's.

We were not the only ones putting a push on. While we worked, carpenters, plumbers, and electricians were working overtime to finish their portion of the job. Overhead, a crane was putting up the big golden arches that mean McDonalds. It was amusing to see the power these arches had to draw in traffic off the highway. As soon as they were up, cars began rolling in one after another. Couples got out, stretched, got the kids out of their car seats and found the doors to the restaurant locked. Puzzled, they would rattle the handles and try to see inside through the glass. We had to explain to them that the restaurant was not quite open yet. The kids were loaded back into the car and all drove away disappointed. Then the next car drove in. All day long.

The McDonald's job marked a turning point in our style of landscape design. We began putting more and more herbaceous perennials into the plantings. Gardeners were asking for perennials. Gardening magazines featured articles on perennial gardening, and plant breeders were rapidly introducing new species and cultivars. Perennials combined well with plantings of trees and shrubs, adding colour and variety; and skilful gardeners could plant them in masses to create beautiful beds just like in the magazines.

Pleasant Valley Nurseries received an important leg-up from the town of Antigonish, which frequently hired us to do work. For a start, we did extensive tree plantings in certain neighbourhoods almost barren of trees. These included Brookland Street and the streets around Arbor Drive, the Heights, and selected spots on Main Street. Every house was to get a tree in the front yard.

We planted maples—also lindens and honey locusts, of which there were few in Antigonish—and some crab apples and birches. Once or twice we got chased away by someone who didn't want a tree in their yard, but most people were happy to have one. It was interesting to observe the different responses of homeowners to their new tree. Some stayed in the house and didn't appear to even notice it. Others, however, rushed out as soon as we moved on, making the circle bigger and putting more soil and fertilizer in it and planting flowers.

Most all the trees planted then are fully grown today, but those with the flower beds around them were noticeably faster-growing. We began, in fact, to recommend to anyone planting a tree that they make the planting spot extra-large, with extra soil and fertilizer, and add a couple of shrubs or some flowers. Trees grew impressively fast this way and began to reverse the pessimistic attitude that there was no point planting trees because you wouldn't live long enough to see them grow. There were soon trees thriving all over town, many of them planted by homeowners who were justly proud of the way they were growing, and eager to plant more.

Bruce Partridge

The town of Port Hawkesbury was good to us through the years as well, and liked our work. Whenever the pulp mill was doing well there was great enthusiasm to dress up the town. We were the recipients of nice contracts to do our part by planting trees and shrubs in key places. Town councillor Doreen Alexander worked tirelessly to promote ornamental plantings and passed much of the work on to us. She especially liked the Austrian pine—which does well in Port Hawkesbury despite the winds and sea spray. Many are still thriving there today. Other town officials, notably Paula Davis and Jim Pyke, promoted us for important plantings.

One of the largest, and just about the most unusual, projects we were ever hired to do was the creation of a park at the intersection of Reeves Street and Granville. The spot was essentially a big hollow exposed to the blast of waves, wind, salty spray and snow from the Strait of Canso. The plan was to fill it with compacted bark peeled from logs at the pulp mill, then cover it with enough topsoil to grow grass and trees. No one was certain that this scheme would work—especially in the case of the trees. We piled the topsoil deeper where the trees would go, but there was some anxiety that they would sink or somehow be poisoned as the bark decomposed underground. Also, there was the question of wind and spray off the strait. We couldn't say no to work, though, and took it on.

Work on the park kept four men busy for a good part of two summers. This included travelling back and forth daily from Antigonish and laying down what seemed like acres of sod. In those days, sod was delivered in rolls—50 on a pallet. A flat-bed truck could carry 20 or more pallets, which had to be unloaded by hand, one roll at a time. We had no way to lift off full pallets. This usually meant two men on the truck passing rolls down to two men on the ground for an hour or two. This went quite routinely if the day was dry and the sods weren't muddy—but usually it wasn't and they were.

Unloading muddy sods in the rain is something you can't forget. For one thing, the sods have sunk on the pallets and are stuck together. It takes quite a pull to get one loose. Then, if you are the guy on the ground, the sod will likely unroll as soon as you take it, and slap you in the face with the muddy end.

When Fall arrived, and colder weather set in, the sods were more likely to be frozen. We worked on that park the first summer until there was snow and it was no longer possible to get sod. By the end we were laying frozen sods on frozen ground. At least a wheelbarrow pushes more easily over ice than it does through the mud.

At the park, we didn't always work alone. Doreen Alexander sometimes provided us with half a dozen or so young offenders who had been convicted of some minor crime, and sentenced to help us lay sod at the park. I guess we were supposed to show them what it meant to do good honest work for a living. These were not particularly bad boys, but for them good honest work was not pushing a heavy wheelbarrow of sod through the mud. They were holding out for something high-paying, easy and clean. We ended up doing most of the work ourselves.

At last, the second summer, we finished up the park before the weather got too bad. We planted maples, ash and birch, which have all done quite well, and the grass is green to this day. It is a good little spot for a picnic across the road from the harbour.

In our heyday, when both the landscapers and the equipment were young, we worked as far west as Pictou and New Glasgow—where for several summers we almost went house to house on Terrace Street. We did a big job in Sydney and travelled frequently to Inverness, and we worked in Canso, which happened to be the easternmost point of mainland North America—as East-coast as you could get.

Before the wireless, Canso was a prime destination for trans-Atlantic cables from Europe. The first cable came into Canso in 1881. News, including both the sinking of the *Titanic* and the stock market crash of 1929, was relayed back and forth from Canso to the rest of the continent until 1955. Canso got news before New York did.

By the time Canso heard of Pleasant Valley Nurseries, the cable was obsolete, but the fishery was still thriving. Our first landscaping work in Canso was an invitation to plant trees and shrubs at the Seaman's memorial—a small park devoted to the memory of Canso's long sad list of lost and drowned mariners. This planting did well, still looks good today, and earned us more work with the town, including planting around the town museum and a nursing home. We also landscaped several private properties in and around the town.

For a few years the drive to the tip of North America was a regular thing. We tried, however, to put off our work in Canso until the last thing in the Fall, when it was too wintry to work in Antigonish. In the summer, Canso was invariably colder than Antigonish, with chill winds blowing off the open Atlantic. More than once, we left the garden centre for Canso in light summer clothes and found ourselves rooting for old jackets and sweatshirts under the seat of the truck once we got there.

Oddly enough, though, because of the proximity to the ocean, things in Canso didn't freeze up as early as they did inland. When it had become too frosty to do any more planting in Antigonish, we still had four or five weeks to work in Canso. We never got tired of the drive, with the rocks and pounding seas of Chedabucto Bay on one side and the ancient dwarf forest and orchid bogs on the other.

When things went well, we made money on landscaping. It was a fine line, though, between making money and losing it. Almost every job required an estimate, and it was very difficult to bill a customer for more than the estimate when things went wrong. Therefore, it was important to consider the job from every angle and try to think of everything before venturing a figure.

It didn't help that those of us doing the figuring were cheapskates ourselves, and shocked at our own estimates. The prices of the plants and materials were pretty easy to add up, but figuring out the hours of labour required was tricky. By the time we added what we thought would be the labour charge to the total, it was getting embarrassing. We were worried that the good people we were working for would suspect that we were taking advantage of them. We wanted to save them money wherever we could. It was very tempting to think that we could reduce the labour part of the job if we just worked harder.

If anything at all went wrong though—and it often did—this approach backfired badly and we ended up working harder for nothing. Henri said that when he was a boy in Holland, workmen presented an itemized bill with individual boxes for labour and materials, and one for profit. We almost felt that we had to keep profit hidden and quiet as if it was unethical to make any. We certainly couldn't spell it out to the dollar. It was a few years and quite a few jobs before we learned to present a realistic estimate without cringing. Eventually, though, we were usually making money, and there was a continuing demand for our services.

Alas, nothing stays good forever. Age and a slowing economy crept up on us. As gardeners became more experienced and capable of doing their own work, demand for our services dropped off. Equipment was wearing out and wasn't worth replacing. It was becoming harder and harder to find young people willing to work at manual labour. It was even harder to find young people interested in plants. Jack, Paul, and Bruce Davidson had gone their separate ways. Henri and I were getting older and Henri's back was giving him trouble. It looked like time to quit.

The question was whether or not the business could survive without landscaping. Until now, a fairly high percentage of plants sold from the garden centre were taken for landscaping, along with large quantities of peat moss, manure and other planting supplies. It was a hard decision. The fact that the truck and equipment were wearing out and crew hard to find helped to tip the scales.

Fortunately, by this time there were several independent landscapers doing good work and we could send people their way. We were on good terms with them, and they bought most of their plants and materials at PVN. The stars were aligned and we hung up the shovels.

As of Spring 2000 there was no more landscaping for Pleasant Valley Nurseries, but there was still the nursery, the greenhouses, and the store.

Bruce Partridge

Digging small trees at the nursery.

The nursery

A nursery was what Henri intended from the beginning. Starting plants from cuttings and seeds was interesting work and required little investment at first. Henri, as a young man, reasoned that if you could start trees and shrubs for next to nothing, grow them up, and sell them for a good price, you should be able to make a living at it. The garden centre on Church St. Extension would be the sales outlet. Pleasant Valley Nurseries would do nothing but grow and sell plants. Today Henri is retired and pleasantly cynical and is happy to recount all the pitfalls he was unaware of back then, and why things were not that simple.

The nursery was by no means a failure. At its peak it was an impressive sight. We raised and sold thousands of trees and shrubs through the garden centre, accounting for a good part of our sales. We purchased the remainder from other nurseries—most grown in the deep soil and sun of Southern Ontario or the USA, where nursery rows stretched from horizon to horizon. Henri's courageous little nursery, begun on worn-out cow pastures first in Pleasant Valley, then in Lakevale, in a region of short summers and cool weather, faced some unique challenges.

Henri had begun the nursery in Pleasant Valley with small maples and lindens and rows of freshly-grafted fruit trees, which were all growing vigorously. The land, however, was steep and stony and difficult to work. We spent many hours digging and planting in the clay and among the rocks. We never dug up some trees because they were too inaccessible and the window for digging in Spring was short. Ideally, tree nurseries are on flat ground with light, stone-free soil. That combination is uncommon in Antigonish County, but Henri was looking.

He found what he was looking for in Lakevale: 75 acres of abandoned fields and cut-over woodland. The fields were flat and, even better, the soil was sandy loam with hardly any rocks. Soon he sold the place in Pleasant Valley and moved his operation, lock, stock and barrel, to Lakevale. He dug a pond and a well, put in a road through the woods, and he and Phyllis were building a house.

He wasted no time plowing up an acre or two and filling it with small trees and evergreens. The fields in Lakevale were flat and the soil was workable. We were improving it rapidly with manures and cover crops and plants were growing well.

Besides good soil, though, a nursery can use some heat. Commercial nurseries in Southern Ontario and throughout the USA can produce an 8-foot, well-branched shade tree or saleable fruit tree in two years after grafting. This was not going to happen in Lakevale. Cool, short summers restricted the growth of trees and a saleable tree took at least one extra year to produce. This, coupled with the fact that we were committed to growing trees from seed, made tree-growing a somewhat lengthy process.

Now, it is a sad fact that a tree doesn't have to be dead to be unsaleable. A perfectly good tree that grows crooked, or has a broken top, or has a branch torn off the side, won't sell. The longer you keep a tree in the nursery, the greater likelihood that something will damage it. Ice, snow, or wind can damage a tree. Machinery can run over it. Mice or rabbits gnaw bark, and the worst is deer.

When Henri was a boy, he worked in nurseries in Holland. He knew how to grow a tree. The trees he had put in that first summer in Lakevale were growing nicely and could be ready for sale next summer, or at least the one after. That is until the deer found them. Deer are lovely creatures, but in late Fall or Winter they visit the nursery. Hungry. And looking to rub their horns. The two things deer like best are grafted fruit trees to eat and lindens upon which to scrape their horns. We had both. They damaged almost everything except evergreens that winter, and the trees would take a couple more years to recover. We didn't see this coming. This nursery business was proving to be a learning experience.

Summer finally brought heat—and black flies. With pruning, some of the fruit trees and lindens would recover. In the meantime, they needed tending. In the big nurseries of Southern Ontario, rows of trees stretch as far as the eye can see in clean soil without a single weed of any kind—thanks to herbicides. Henri and Phyllis were not keen on using herbicides, or pesticides of any kind, for that matter, on their property, and weeds in the nursery grew with gay abandon. Everyone pulled weeds. If the landscapers were caught up with landscaping work, they were at the nursery pulling weeds. Along with eating and breathing black flies, we kept weeds in check, but this was more money invested that we might never see again.

Shrubs on a capillary bed.

We didn't give up, and began to work things out bit by bit. The deer had not touched the evergreens in the nursery—pines, spruces, and junipers— and they were looking good. We began to dig them and take them to the garden centre. They were healthy and nicely shaped and we were proud to be selling them.

As for the deciduous trees, we built fenced-in growing areas where only the craziest high-jumping deer ever got in and trees could grow in relative safety. There was also a good crop of dwarf evergreens and flowering shrubs that we had started from cuttings and were growing in pots. Such a good crop, in fact, that keeping them watered began to be a problem and a chore.

Growing shrubs or trees in containers was just beginning to be common in the nursery trade and Henri was studying the techniques and talking to other growers. He decided to build a capillary bed, one answer to the problem of watering a large number of plants growing in pots. It was an area of sand underlaid with perforated water pipes, then meticulously raked and levelled. The potted shrubs were set out over this area and spaced just far enough apart to give them room to grow. When the irrigation water flowed onto the sand beds it rose by capillary action to water the shrubs through the holes in the bottoms of the pots. This worked well, and the capillary bed covered with growing trees and shrubs was an impressive sight. A step forward.

In small-town Nova Scotia, you can't make a living doing just one thing. Country people here have traditionally fished and farmed in the summer, and worked in the woods during the winter. Similarly, we looked to diversify. Around 1980, the Christmas tree and blueberry industries in the province were taking off, and Henri reasoned that maybe there was a market for starter seedlings to supply the growers. Thus began the balsam fir-growing phase of Pleasant Valley Nurseries—a very bold and memorable enterprise, indeed.

We did experiment with growing blueberry plants from seed, and grew some nice ones, but it soon came to be all balsam fir. We started the fir from seed in trays, then moved them into nursery beds for a year or two.

Since no one sold balsam fir seed, we had to get our own. In the woods in late August and September, the fir cones are ripe. They stand upright in the treetops like purple candles dripping with balsam. The Minister of Lands and Forests gave a permission letter to harvest seed anywhere on Crown land, so once we had located an area with cone-bearing fir that were not too tall, in we went with our buckets and ladders.

Picking cones meant getting completely covered in balsam. Our hands and gloves were so covered that we couldn't drop the cones into the bucket. Just try rooting a black fly out of your ear with a finger like that! Our hair was gobbed up and our eyelids stuck open. At the end of the day, we cleaned our hands in gasoline. We hid our ladders in the woods 'til tomorrow, and dragged the cones to the truck.

Back at the garden centre, we dumped the cones out of the bags into an empty greenhouse to dry. When they were dry, we broke the cones up and crumbled them into a mixture of seeds and chaff which we shovelled into bags. Henri drove the bags of dried and broken-up cones to a seed-cleaning facility in Fredericton where they could separate the seed from the chaff. The cleaned seed came back to Antigonish.

Jason Steeghs in the cone-drying shed.

We kept some of the seed—maybe half—to start our own fir seedlings to sell to the growers. The rest we offered to seed companies in Canada and the United States. Americans were growing fir

Christmas trees themselves, but they liked the strain that grew in Nova Scotia. They called it "double balsam" for its heavily-needled branches, and were interested in seed. For a couple of years Henri took cross-border drives during the off-season, delivering seed. Cone-picking went on for a week or two, and in those years we pickers looked forward to it as a break from the usual routine.

At home, beds of sturdy-looking fir seedlings were growing nicely in Lakevale. Local tree growers were receptive and willing to try them out. The trouble was, the little trees had to be dug out of the ground to be sold. This was only possible in the Spring or the Fall. In between, small trees couldn't be moved.

Nishula rolls.

Then we discovered the Nishula roll—an innovation from Finland. The Nishula roll was a strip of white plastic film about 12 inches wide and six feet long which you rolled out on a long table and covered with an inch or so of good growing mix. Two workers stood, one on each side of the table, putting in fir seedlings while a third rolled the plastic up and taped it closed. The result was a cylinder of plastic with little trees sticking out of either end. We cut the cylinder in half to yield two rolls and stood the rolls on the ground, tree side up.

In the Spring, we did hundreds and hundreds of these rolls. If you didn't take care to keep busy, you'd get sent to do Nishula rolls.

After rolling, little trees grew for another season and then we sold them to growers. The rolls were easy to handle and could be unrolled and the seedlings planted even in mid-summer, since it wasn't necessary to cut or otherwise disturb the root system. Henri had figured out a reasonable price to charge for a roll of trees, and tree growers were happy to get them.

But then the government of Nova Scotia decided to get into the act.

Having observed that Christmas tree growing was becoming an important industry in the province, and reneging on their promise to leave balsam fir growing to private growers, the Department of Lands and Forests began producing seedlings at their state-of-the-art, taxpayer subsidized, tree-growing facilities in Lawrencetown. They were equipped to grow mass quantities and offer them generously to growers at a lower price than we were asking.

At home, to make things worse, a flock of grosbeaks descended on our handsome little trees, taking the terminal bud out of every one. A double blow that spelled the end of over ten years of balsam fir seedlings at Pleasant Valley Nurseries.

One good thing that came out of the Nishula roll experience was that we learned how to formulate a good, inexpensive growing mixture for plants in containers. After much experimentation, Henri developed a growing mix that performed very well and was based upon rotted sawdust and bark with added limestone, fertilizers and minerals. Rotted sawdust and bark were available in large quantities at local sawmills, and provided a relatively inexpensive base for big batches of mix. This became our "secret formula" in which we grew shrubs and trees nicely in pots right up until the end.

We were sometimes aghast at the growing mixes other nurseries used, and occasionally had to smugly re-pot their plants into our own mix. Springtime each year we spent a couple of days making up a summer's worth.

At the end of the balsam fir era, we were specializing in native tree species grown from seed and choice evergreen shrub varieties from cuttings. We had come to realize that native tree species were invariably more dependable than imports, though it seems to be human nature to always want what you don't have. In Europe the birches, oaks and maples that grow everywhere here are prized as beautiful exotics.

Nursery evergreens.

Despite our noble posturing, we also admired and sold many species native to Europe and Asia. It is hard to resist gems like Japanese maple, magnolia or Chinese dogwood, or the colourful varieties of Norway maple (Crimson King, Princeton Gold, etc.), all of which do well here. But we unfailingly trusted in the native species for core planting around properties, along with which we might plant other species for variety and added interest. We were pleased to be able to offer trees grown from seed, which, in the long run, were stronger and longer-lived than their grafted counterparts.

Dwarf evergreens such as creeping spruce, juniper, false cypress, cedar and yew, in their myriad sizes, shapes and colours, were a popular item at the garden centre. Broadleaf evergreens—particularly rhododendrons and azaleas—also were in great demand. We started all of these from cuttings usually taken in winter and rooted inside greenhouses in a bed of sand with heat underneath and a mist of water overhead to prevent wilting. We first potted the rooted cuttings in tiny pots and then moved them up to larger ones as they grew. The goal was to produce a saleable evergreen in a one- or two-gallon pot. Some of these evergreens grew only a few inches a year, so this process could take four or five years and lots of transplanting.

Eventually, though, the years passed, the evergreens grew, and we had the rooting process streamlined. The capillary beds outside filled up with homegrown evergreens ready to go—more, unfortunately, than we were going to be able to sell.

Once you have perfected growing a certain plant, it is very easy to grow too many. This is not immediately obvious, though, when the plant takes years to grow. For a while, it looked as if the nursery was going to carry the business. Maybe we could quit landscaping. We were bringing in truckloads of trees and shrubs from Lakevale to sell in town. The sums were heady and Henri quite euphoric.

Somehow, though—a chastened Henri will tell you today—it didn't quite add up. If the years of work and materials necessary to produce these loads were added to the cost of surplus plants that couldn't be sold, margins were surprisingly slim.

The nursery helped us to earn a living, but we kept on landscaping.

Henri still keeps a nursery in Lakevale and is still growing trees. He is propagating varieties of American elm resistant to the Dutch elm disease and trying to re-establish the elm in our area. He is also trying to find and graft disease-resistant specimens of American beech—once a very valuable tree in our forests.

Bruce Partridge

Looking back at Pleasant Valley Nurseries, he is likely to recount wryly his gradual realization that Phyllis and the girls in the greenhouse could grow a hanging basket in six weeks and sell it for the same price as his four-year-old tree. This fact was not lost on Phyllis either, and Pleasant Valley Nurseries took another fork in the road.

Digging and potting spruces at the nursery.

The greenhouses

This fork led towards more intensive and imaginative use of the greenhouses. Starved for the sight of flowers after a long cold winter, gardeners in Nova Scotia were attracted to greenhouses like bears to honey.

Spring inside the greenhouse.

Spring inside the greenhouse was a far cry from Spring outside—which could usually be classified as raw. The warmth and the colour and the smell of growing things were irresistible, and customers wanted to take it all home. We were forever telling them that it was still too cold outside for flowers and that they would have to wait. Not to be deterred, many paid for the baskets and planters they fancied and left them with us until time to take them home.

Shoppers were in a good mood, paid little attention to prices, and seemed to regard any outlay on flowers as money well spent. This made it easy for us and was a pleasant contrast to landscape or tree and shrub customers, who seemed to examine every penny.

We sold nearly everything we had in the greenhouse by August and we were left wishing we had more to sell. Phyllis began bringing in a much wider variety of greenhouse plants, which the workers arranged into ever larger and lovelier baskets and planters. The writing was on the wall.

Through the late 80s and early 90s at PVN, while sales of trees and shrubs levelled off, greenhouse sales continued to climb. The town of Antigonish began to commission large hanging baskets and planters to dress up the Main.

Beautifying downtown Ryan Gillis photo
More than 100 flower baskets from Pleasant Valley Nurseries, which will be placed along Main Street in Antigonish, received some final touches from Henri Steeghs and Janette Fecteau recently. The colorful baskets will be hung this Saturday in an effort to make the downtown area more attractive in the summer months.

At its peak, the garden centre featured large greenhouses on either side of the store stuffed with hanging baskets and flowers for sale, as well as three smaller greenhouses for holding surplus stock and immature plants. Still, in May and June, we couldn't keep them full. Phyllis kept a steady supply of replacement plants and baskets growing in the greenhouses in Lakevale, which Henri ferried into town daily. The nurseryman was now a flower man, too.

Hanging baskets for the town of Antigonish.

From the start, we used greenhouses at the garden centre to house and display the annual flowers, vegetable transplants, and tender perennials that we sold, as well as planters and hanging baskets. We outgrew the original little wooden hoop house of the 70s very quickly.

Our assumption was that we would build a larger wooden greenhouse, but Henri surprised us by ordering a beautiful fifty-foot by fifty-foot, heavy-duty, galvanized-steel structure from a greenhouse company. It featured four attractive arched bays supported by iron posts set in concrete. Trouble was, it came in pieces.

Bruce Partridge

The arched bays were a loose jumble of nuts and bolts and pipe, and we would have to set the posts.

The first steel greenhouses

Three of us, who had scarcely even built a doghouse but were young enough to try anything, set to work in the mud with a rented level and post-hole digger and got it done. With the plastic in place, it was quite elegant and a beautiful space to fill with flowers. When it was cold outside in Spring, everyone loved the smell of flowers and the warmth. We even began to get school tours.

A new invention for greenhouses at the time, was the use of two layers of plastic on the roof with air blown in between to inflate them a couple of inches apart. Surprisingly, this only required a tiny fan—like a little bathroom fan—and worked perfectly. It gave the whole building a shiny, rounded appearance from the outside. In addition, it decreased heat loss dramatically and kept the plastic tight and resistant to flapping in the wind. We were quite proud of our new greenhouse. Never wasteful, we moved the old wooden one out back to grow roses.

The first four or five years in town, potted flowers and transplants in our new greenhouse came mostly from Duykers' greenhouses in Afton or in crates from Holland. Before long, we put up a hundred-foot production greenhouse in Lakevale, where we began to grow our own annuals and perennials to bring into the garden centre to sell.

In 'the biosphere'.

Soon we were running out of space in town, so, one after another, we set up three fifty-foot houses in the lower part of the yard to hold the overflow. We also covered these with double plastic that we inflated. Though only one was heated—we called it the "geranium house"—they were all stuffed with plants. In Fall, we covered the three houses with white plastic to keep out the sun and used them to winter left-over stock.

The last greenhouse to go up at PVN, in 2001, was a lovely state-of-the-art one-hundred-footer on the opposite side of the store from the first one. This greenhouse, dubbed the "biosphere", was another prime sales area, and held geraniums and begonias from Lakevale as well as petunias and other annual flowers and vegetable transplants. We hung large, intricately-beautiful hanging baskets, most planted up for Main Street Antigonish, from pipes on the ceiling.

Once again, this greenhouse arrived in pieces and we put it together ourselves. We were pretty good at it by this time, and with five greenhouses on the property we were a serious plant business. To this day, we are indebted to the many avid gardeners who were as serious as we were and made us their first stop for summer flowers.

Beverly, Linda, and Janette, pillars of PVN.

Looking back on it, the success of our greenhouses could be attributed to two things—the greenhouse women, and the greenhouse mix. Men were outside in the yard or working on the landscape crew and not often in the greenhouse anyway. It was the women who kept greenhouses stocked and attractive, and the plants healthy, and who planted up all the hanging baskets and containers.

These women were on their feet all day, planting and moving plants around. Also, they had to be artistic and have a thorough knowledge of the habits and growing requirements of plants. For example, you cannot mix sun-lovers and shade-lovers in the same container, and it was necessary to know which was which.

Combinations of plants in arrangements became more colourful and complex each year, and the women outdid themselves filling the greenhouses. In addition, appreciative customers and businesses brought back last year's empties for us to refill with fresh soil and replant. These were invariably large and heavy, and we moved most of them to the lower greenhouses to grow and fill out. The women had to lift them all over again when the cars and trucks came to pick them up. Just to make things interesting, they had to somehow accomplish all this work while cheerfully showing customers around and answering questions.

A list of all the women and young girls that handled the greenhouses is a long one, but several names stand out. Yvonne MacDonald (later Yvonne Maas), started as a young plant science student and kept the greenhouse clean and fresh by hosing down the concrete walkways every morning. Linda Petite, Beverley Fraser, and Holly Chisholm came later as young women to keep the expanding greenhouses full and beautiful, and to make a career at Pleasant Valley Nurseries. Phyllis, of course, was there from start to finish.

There was always one young woman tending the production greenhouses in Lakevale while everyone else was at the garden centre. This was a different kettle of fish altogether. Lakevale isn't as placid as it sounds. Holly, Janette or Julia can tell you what it was like to be working alone while a bear roamed just on the other side of the plastic. There were a few terror-stricken phone calls to

Henri in town, but fortunately all the bears wandered off on their own.

Holly watering.

We deeply appreciated and trusted the women we had working in our greenhouses, and relied upon them to keep the greenhouses running smoothly year after year, to handle customers, and to make work easier for the rest of us.

The second secret to our success was PVN's invention of the greenhouse mix. No matter how artistic and inspired the plant arrangement, it has to grow. We had tried a variety of commercially-prepared planting mixes, but found them always somewhat short on nutrients. Before long, we had to supplement all the planters and hanging baskets with water-soluble fertilizer. This was time-consuming, tedious, and, with so many things to fertilize, rather hit or miss. We began to work on a growing mix of our own.

Manufacturing greenhouse mix.

The result was our soon-to-be-famous GH, or greenhouse mix. We also did an HP for house plants. We based both, and all our other growing mixes, on peat moss, but incorporated limestone, trace elements, bone meal, coated slow-release fertilizers, and even compost. Once we got the proportions figured out, plants in our greenhouses grew magnificently. We used the mix for perennials, which loved it also. When we used this mix in containers, plants could grow and bloom nicely all summer with minimum additional fertilizer.

Customers caught on, and were soon asking to buy greenhouse mix to use at home. After a while we could barely keep up. The men and women at the garden centre were kept busy mixing and bagging. The last few years that we were in business, one young man, Leif Watson, spent hours a day in a dust mask doing almost nothing else. It's no wonder he quit to work elsewhere.

Between customers and ourselves, we went through mountains of the stuff. Henri and Phyllis were also using it in the greenhouses in Lakevale. If for nothing else, I think Pleasant Valley Nurseries will always be remembered in Antigonish for the greenhouse mix. Sometimes it seemed as if we could close the rest of the place down and do nothing but manufacture GH.

As beautiful as they are, operating greenhouses is no easy matter. From the time we started them up in Spring until we closed them up in Fall, Henri and Phyllis didn't sleep very well. In the cold weather of late winter into Spring, we heated the greenhouses with oil furnaces. When the temperature outside was well below freezing and the nights were long, or on cloudy days, the furnaces ran constantly and required a lot of oil. This expense was unfortunate, but expected, and that wasn't what worried Henri and Phyllis.

What was worse, and always a danger, was a power outage or an equipment breakdown. Either one could shut down the furnaces and destroy an entire greenhouse full of plants in a very short time. The heating system for the growing greenhouses in Lakevale was complex and required water lines, pumps and valves. Any of these things could, and did, fail, and nothing would work in a power outage.

Henri was checking constantly on the greenhouses during the day, and in and out of bed at night. He had a generator gassed up and ready to go at all times. The greenhouses in Lakevale, and those in town were equipped with alarms that were supposed to alert Henri to a sudden drop in temperature, but couldn't be trusted.

The alarms in town were the worst. These were hooked up to ring Henri's phone at home to wake him up. A robotic voice came on to inform him that there was "low temperature in greenhouse 1", or wherever the problem was. In the coldest weather, these alarms were not infrequent, and could be expected in the dead of night. Most were false alarms, but Henri took the midnight drives an hour into town and back because he couldn't afford to take a chance. On nights that the alarm didn't ring, he still lost sleep fearing that it would.

In the greenhouse, when the weather warmed up and the furnaces were no longer necessary, plants grew happily in the warmth and the miraculous GH mix. So did the diseases and bugs. These could wreak havoc if we did not detect them in time. In the early years we were inexperienced and sometimes taken by surprise. Spider mites, aphids, white fly, mealy bugs and various rots and mildews showed up to teach us a lesson.

We lost plants but got smarter. We began to know what to look for and what to expect, and began to fight back. We found that if we caught problems early, we could cope using harmless dusts and sprays. We released predatory insects into the greenhouses to fight fire with fire, and we developed an eagle eye for developing problems. Linda, Beverly, Holly or Phyllis could spot insects and diseases from a mile away.

As the cool Spring moved into Summer, greenhouses heated up. Cooling and watering became the problem. On a sunny day, temperatures inside could shoot up to lethal levels very quickly. Actually, this could happen on a sunny day in winter, too, but the greenhouses were not usually full of plants then. Inside the Summer greenhouse, plants dried out quickly and needed watering several times a day.

All the greenhouses were built to be cooled in hot weather. Some had big fans blowing out hot air and sucking in cool outside air through vents, while others had sides that could be rolled up to allow air flow from outside. In our unpredictable Spring weather, we sometimes were turning fans on and off and rolling vents up and down all on the same day. This worked well as long as staff was at the garden centre. The problem was after mid-summer, when we were closing at 5 and closed on Sundays. The sun was still high at 5 and the fans had to be on and the vents open. It could cool off quickly, though, after dark, and someone, usually Henri or Phyllis, had to stop in to close them up. Sundays, someone had to come in early to open vents and water. Beverly lived in town and often did this. Sunday evening, greenhouses had to be closed up again and plants watered once more. This evening visit usually fell to Henri or Phyllis. You can understand why they were relieved when, in August, the greenhouses were finally empty and they could get a full night's sleep.

A dreaded job was putting new plastic on the greenhouses before the old plastic wore out. New plastic came in enormous sheets of 100 feet long and 30 or 40 feet wide, in a big heavy roll. A house required two full sheets when it was re-done, one sheet on top of the other so we could blow air in between for the reasons I explained earlier. Greenhouse plastic was UV protected to resist breaking down in sunlight, and was good for four years. Those four years went surprisingly quickly, and it seemed that every year there were at least a couple of houses whose time was up. Even though the old plastic might seem to be as good as ever, it had to come off. We couldn't take the chance of losing a greenhouse full of plants if it all went to pieces.

It was time to pay attention to the wind. To put a new covering of plastic on the greenhouse, the wind had to be dead calm. A 40x100 foot sheet of plastic catches a lot of wind and a breeze getting under it was likely to lift it, and anyone hanging on, clear across the highway.

One of our summer workers, Sean Chisholm, and I, once proved this in a spectacular way. We were taking the plastic off the flat roof of a shade house that had been covered for the winter. The roof was made of 2x4s on edge 2 feet apart. The plastic was held down by laths nailed through the plastic into these 2x4s. The wind was brisk that day and it was not easy, standing with one leg on one board and one on another, pulling up the laths with our hammers. We should have waited for a still day, but I thought if we took the laths off the top and left the ones around the edges, the plastic would stay put while we climbed down and finished the job from the ground.

Not so.

As we stood on the middle of the roof pulling off the last laths, a huge gust of wind tore the entire sheet loose. It shot straight up into the air, lifting Sean and me off our feet and dropping us sideways back onto the roof. Stunned and completely wrapped in plastic, we couldn't see where we were coming down and landed hard on the 2x4s. We untangled ourselves and got off the building with painfully bruised ribs but no broken bones.

I felt justifiably stupid and sorry for Sean because it had been my big idea. Another painful lesson, and I was careful never to go flying on a sheet of plastic again.

Early morning was almost always the best time to attempt the plastic because the wind was still, but there was always the danger that it could pick up while we had the sheet draped across the greenhouse framework but before we had fastened it down. Bitter experience taught us that if this happened, we might as well pull the plastic down and try another day rather than wrestle with it. Wrestling plastic in the wind was a match we couldn't win.

On the positive side, with experience, we learned to change the plastic quickly and have it fastened down enough to be safe in two hours or less, with all of us working. Still, those two hours were nerve wracking, with everyone on high alert for any trace of wind. You may wonder how anyone could be stressed in a garden centre, but I managed it every time we had to change plastic. Over the dozens of occasions that we changed greenhouse plastic, we were careful to choose our day and actually seldom failed, but we always worried about it.

Once we had the plastic fastened down sufficiently to be out of danger, there were still hours of tedious work fastening it down completely, installing vents, and trimming off excess plastic. At home, I made sure that I built my greenhouse of glass.

Bruce Partridge

The store

If we weren't working on the greenhouses, we were working on the store. By the "store" I mean the garden centre building on Church St. Extension.

Henri's original little building (20 x 20 ft.) was too small almost at once. There was no room for an office and, worse, no bathroom. By the third Spring, 1980, we had added on another piece towards the back using railroad ties, rough lumber and rustic cedar shingles, as was our style. At least this time we had electricity to run our saws. This new addition gave us the long-awaited bathroom, a lunch room, and a bit of office space, as well as room to do landscape designs.

Still crowded, but we made do until 1984 when we added the third and final addition on the back—right up to the property line. This addition became the official office. Again, we built on railroad ties and tried to mimic the rest of the building.

All three pieces were attached to one another and did indeed look like a single structure, except that each piece settled differently. This gave the roof an unusual three-stepped appearance which we eventually concealed with a level bed of strapping over the whole thing, and steel roofing.

Henri loved the nursery, some of us loved the greenhouses, no one loved landscaping, but we all loved the store. This was the heart and soul of the operation. No matter what we were doing, we started out there in the morning and finished up there at the end of the day. Everything grown at the nursery or in the greenhouses in Lakevale came there to be sold.

The garden centre building was handmade and cute and attached to the two big sales greenhouses on either side. Around the building and across the drive we displayed all the colourful trees and shrubs that we were hoping to sell. There was a pond to display water plants. There were shade structures for shade-loving plants. We worked constantly to keep the plants healthy and attractively arranged.

At the garden centre we could show off. We were all gardeners and grew gardens of our own. We were graduates of horticulture school. We knew the Latin names of plants. We had worked in the nursery and in the greenhouses and on the landscaping crew. We had read. We had kept our eyes open. We were eager to help and to advise customers who came with their questions, and we all liked one another. We worked as a team.

Linda Petite at the counter.

Customers, mostly gardeners themselves, came to wander the grounds and greenhouses, shop, chat and ask questions. Our job, and we took it seriously, was to offer our knowledge and experience to help select plants. This was often an interesting quest involving the colour of the plant or flowers, evergreen or deciduous, blooming time, height desired, sun or shade, wet ground or dry, exposure to wind, snow cover, fragrance, edibility and so on.

Other businesses sold many of the same plants that we did, but they couldn't offer this type of service. Old customers I run into on the street almost universally say that the thing they miss most about Pleasant Valley Nurseries is the good information and advice they got there.

Now and then there was someone with enough nerve to phone us up about a plant they had purchased elsewhere, and could we tell them how to plant it. Well, we rolled our eyes plenty but went ahead and told them. Maybe they would buy it from us next time.

Customers appreciated our advice and we made friends who came to our garden centre year after year. We helped many get started with gardening and we enjoyed their successes.

This was not at all a one-way street, however. There were things to learn from every customer. Things they had tried and what had worked and what hadn't. This added greatly to our store of knowledge and we dutifully passed it on to other gardeners. Members of the Antigonish and other regional garden clubs visited regularly and we learned from them. Pleasant Valley Nurseries was truly a hub of avid gardening. PVN was a good place to appreciate plants. Henri and Phyllis brought in stock from all across Canada and the USA—anything that was likely to grow in our climate.

In addition, customers often arrived with mysterious plants found in their gardens or in the woods, to have them identified. This became a fun game we called "name that plant". This game sometimes involved the staff squinting and scratching their heads, trying to figure it out from pictures in the books we kept under the counter. We solved tough cases by consulting the "Flora"[1]. Needless

---

1 *The Flora of Nova Scotia*, A.E. Roland, and E.C. Smith

to say, we knew the plant the next time we saw it, and eventually there wasn't much we couldn't identify.

PVN was also a nice place to visit. People enjoyed walking around and exploring. There were the greenhouses, there were all the plants for sale outside, there were mature plantings, there were birds, there was the pond.

The little pond at Pleasant Valley Nurseries was a wonderful thing and lots of fun. I don't think there was a single customer who ever came into the yard without pausing at the pond to check it out. It was irresistible to both frogs and children. I don't know where they came from but it was full of frogs.

If we had allowed, it would have been full of children, too, and we knew where they came from. As families drove into the yard, car doors flew open and kids streaked for the pond, parents right behind trying to catch them by the back of the shirt. It was tough to keep them out of the water, but those were the rules. They retaliated by tossing in any rocks or scraps of wood they could get their hands on when we weren't looking. The frogs never said a thing.

The frogs—big glossy green specimens—sat on the lily pads just like in the storybooks. We used the pond to display the aquatic plants we had for sale, and this included iris and lilies, water hyacinth, arrowhead and others. For several years there were goldfish in the pond, though the water at its deepest was only a little over a foot. When winter came, we were sure the pond would freeze right to the bottom and kill the fish, but we underestimated the goldfish. They must have burrowed into the mud, or maybe there was a little unfrozen water, but next spring, there they were. They were even breeding—there were babies. Tragically, we decided to flush the pond with clean water one day, forgetting that it was town water and chlorinated. That was the end of the fish and their babies, and we never got around to stocking it again.

Nevertheless, the pond, built in an unused corner of the parking lot, was a solid attraction and made the garden centre more fun to visit. There were the permanent plantings of water-loving plants—notably ferns, iris, and ornamental grasses—all around the inside of the rustic fence. There were two tiny waterfalls spilling into the pond which sparkled and splashed. There was a bench to sit on. It was a peaceful place to hang out while the gardener of the family shopped for plants.

Nature was never far away at the garden centre. Plantings at the pond matured and spread on their own. We had permanent plantings of trees and shrubs that looked better every year and added to the allure of the place. Birds adopted the garden centre and nested in our evergreens. Jays dropped acorns and we found little oaks growing where none of us had planted them. Song sparrows sang sweetly from earliest Spring. Bald eagles soared overhead, as did ospreys flying from the West River carrying fish in their talons like torpedoes. Once a snapping turtle as big as a garbage can lid somehow came up from the river to squat on our doorstep. Henri called Bob Bancroft, who came and turned it around facing the river, and the next day it was gone.

Bruce Partridge

Amy van den Hoogen can tell you about the day the mother black duck brought her brood to the garden centre and the cute little things got all scattered and lost among the rows of shrubs. Fearing that one would get run over by a car, Amy and the others working that day, along with helpful customers, herded wild little ducklings around for an hour or more and finally back to their mother, who, thoroughly beside herself, returned with them to the river. As far as I know, they never came back for a visit.

We had mockingbirds nesting one summer and Henri saw a cardinal. Hummingbirds were attracted to the colourful flowers, as were butterflies and bees. Sometimes a hummingbird became trapped in the greenhouse and it was necessary to catch him with our hands or in a net. This could be quite a chase and was extremely entertaining for any children who happened to be in with their parents. Once caught, and examined by the children, we released the tiny little thing outside and it would take off like a rocket.

Borderline Hardy in 5b

The yard itself—basically every area around the pond and the store that could be pressed into service—was also something customers enjoyed. The yard was where we displayed most of the hardy plants we offered for sale, including shade trees, big and small evergreens, broadleaf evergreens, flowering shrubs, fruit trees and fruit bushes, roses and perennials as well as stacks of bagged peat moss and manure. In later years we built a small bamboo shelter from which we sold shade-loving perennials and ferns.

Further up the drive we had a much larger, more formal shade house where we displayed anything we wanted to protect from the sun. Around the pond were the shade trees attached to racks so they wouldn't blow over, larger deciduous shrubs, roses, fruit trees and fruit bushes. Broadleaf evergreens were along one side of the store where they were mostly in the shade.

We kept the front of the store decked out with hardy flowers, with particularly choice perennials and shrubs, as well as anything that happened to be in bloom or was otherwise irresistible. These things either sold fast or went out of bloom and had to be moved, so our displays were constantly changing. Henri regularly brought in fresh new stock from the greenhouses and nursery in Lakevale to replace the plants that were sold, and stock came in from other nurseries. We rearranged the yard daily. This included days when you were off work, so you often returned to find that you didn't know where anything was anymore. Someone had rearranged it.

We displayed herbaceous perennials on benches alongside the store, and they became a very large part of our business starting in the early 80s. We sold a few common ones from the very start, such as day lily, iris, columbine and bleeding heart, but the world of hardy perennials is huge and we were just getting started.

In the 80s, gardeners were becoming rapidly more sophisticated, reading books and magazines, bored with annuals, and asking for perennials. The Antigonish Garden Club was started in 1983, and united many of these people into a gardening awakening that was taking off across the Maritimes.

At the garden centre, Phyllis, especially, noticed this trend, and pushed hard for a more comprehensive selection. At first, we raised perennials from seed, but soon began bringing in more exotic selections that could only be grown from cuttings or division. Plant breeders all across the continent got into the act, introducing myriads of new species and cultivars each year. Before long we had benches of perennials for sale, from creeping thyme and phlox to giant rudbeckia and delphinium, as well as pots of native wildflowers. There were perennials for sun, for shade, for dry spots, for wet spots, Spring bloomers, Summer bloomers, Fall bloomers, perennials to attract birds, perennials to attract butterflies, and they all survived the winter to get bigger and better each year.

Why then, would anyone bother to plant annuals? Annuals were expensive and died over the winter and had to be planted all over again next Summer. Well, here was the catch: once annuals come into bloom, they bloom all summer. Perennials, though, bloom for only a few weeks. Some bloom in the Spring, some in the Summer, and some in the Fall.

Perennial gardening requires planning and skill. It is a matter of choosing and planting varieties that bloom at different times and look good together. Most perennials have good-looking leaves that make up for their short blooming period and the goal is to keep the bed full and the ground covered while having something blooming at every season. This challenge appeals to those who really enjoy gardening and like to grow a variety of different plants.

You can garden with perennials all your life and never run out of new ones to try. We all studied up on perennials and planted them ourselves, and enjoyed offering solid advice and an impressive selection of plants.

Business-wise, herbaceous perennials were a good thing. Most were easy to produce and reasonably priced. Customers weren't deterred by the price of a perennial, and if they bought eight or ten, as many did, it was the same as selling a tree. Gardeners came in looking for perennials and often bought a tree as well. Perennials brought a lot more people to PVN and helped keep us in business after the Spring rush. Furthermore, they were hardy and, if they didn't sell the first Summer, could be kept over to sell the next. They rarely failed to please.

Hardy roses were also somewhat of a specialty at Pleasant Valley Nurseries. We massed them in groups in front of low fences behind the pond. When they all came into bloom in June, it was an impressive site, and most of them were fragrant. We put them on special when they were looking good and they were very popular with our customers.

Each of us at the garden centre had our favourites and would promote them if we were asked. I liked any Rugosa rose, and most Rugosa hybrids. They were hardy and fragrant with healthy, glossy foliage. They had nice Fall colour and attractive fruits or hips. Some grew tall, some sprawled, and some grew in-between. If you had a sunny spot you could pick one for just about any situation. They were practically immune to winter kill and customers had good luck with them.

Of course, Phyllis brought in many other varieties of hardy roses —some hardier than others—with desirable attributes of their own. We all had to learn what to say about these. They were invariably beautiful, anyway, and almost impossible to resist when in bloom.

I had to laugh, though, when Henri looked over a nice group of roses, feigning a puzzled look and asking, "Something's wrong here —where are the aphids?"

Every variety of cultivated rose has a name, and sometimes those will make you laugh. Every Fall, we loaded all the roses we had left into the empty cold storage to keep them over the winter. The cold storage was insulated, and in winter was cold enough to keep the roses dormant but warm enough that they wouldn't freeze.

When Spring came we pulled the roses outside and sorted them. We cut back the good-looking ones and put them out for sale. We divided the rest between those that would go to rehabilitation and those that would go to the dump. One year the last two roses to escape the dump—misshapen, ugly, and nearly dead—bore the tags Carefree Beauty and Hope for Humanity.

Bruce Partridge

Henri and I spent much time out in the yard, moving shade trees and shrubs around and rearranging fruit trees. Fruit trees were something else we specialized in at PVN. Henri's very first foray into the nursery business in Nova Scotia involved growing and grafting apple trees.

We had a large selection. Besides apple trees from our nursery in Lakevale, we had trees from other nurseries including pears, cherries, peaches and plums. Some years we sold uncommon fruits such as apricot, nectarine, quince, and fig, as well as mulberries and nut trees.

There was a lot to take into account when selling a fruit tree. Rootstocks, cultural requirements, hardiness, time of bloom and compatibility for pollination all had to be considered, as well as the fruit characteristics of every variety. Henri and I kept abreast of this and helped gardeners select trees that should be successful in their orchards. Others at the garden centre were as well-informed as we were but were often busy in the store and sent customers out to us.

When he wasn't working with the landscaping crew, Jack MacLeod was the man to ask about fruit trees. He took a consuming interest in learning everything he could about them and eventually quit landscaping to plant his own commercial orchard in Lanark. We were fortunate to know Jack because we could skip the internet and get the lowdown on any fruit tree question straight from him.

Our fruit tree selection was the best anywhere east of the Annapolis valley, and we knew what to say about what we had. Customers frequently reported to me how well their fruit trees had grown since buying them at Pleasant Valley Nurseries.

The garden centre store was where Pleasant Valley Nurseries met the public, and the place to test out and sell anything garden-related. Inside were seeds and seed starting supplies, bulbs, books, birdhouses, fertilizers and pest control products, garden furniture and a hundred other odds and ends that a gardener might need. We had informative pamphlets to give away and a bulletin board to post notices and posters for gardening or community events.

Borderline Hardy in 5b

CBC radio was always on. This was fortunate the day CBC personalities Linden MacIntyre and Carol Off dropped in to buy trees. As It Happened, Carol noticed the radio right away and became very chatty with the girls in the store.

Probably the most ambitious and unlikely product we ever attempted to sell was the rototiller. Early on, in an attempt to diversify, we landed a dealership. We would be selling the prestigious Troy-bilt brand of tiller, which was widely advertised in gardening magazines. The Troy-bilt was a new concept at the time, having the revolving tines behind the wheels and supposedly making it much smoother to operate than front-tine tillers, which could tear your arms right out of their sockets.

The Troy-bilt was a lovely piece of equipment, and looked great parked inside the store. Flaming red in colour, it came in two models, the Pony, and the Horse. The Horse was truly a powerful beast, four hundred pounds of cast iron with a 6 or 7 horsepower engine.

Bruce Partridge

Tines in the rear and self-propelled, it could still tear your arms out of their sockets. In stone-free soil, however, you could indeed walk along beside it holding on with one hand while it made a perfect seedbed—just like in the pictures.

At that time, we were the only business selling the Troy-bilt tiller in our area, and there was a small but steady demand from serious gardeners willing to pay the price.

The tillers came to us in a box and required assembly. This job fell to the landscape crew who were plant guys—not mechanics. We had to bolt the handles on and hook up cables and fill the engine and gearbox with oil. So far so good. But then we also had to assemble the tine clusters and bolt them on. This was a comical nightmare. The instructions explained how to make up three A gangs and one B gang and bolt them on just so underneath the tiller. We were forever getting our gangs mixed up or bolting the whole works onto the tiller backwards. It taxed us landscapers almost to the limits of our mechanical abilities but we eventually got it right. Purchasers were thrilled with their new machines and had no inkling of our struggles in the back shop.

We only sold the Troy-bilt for a few years before better mechanically-equipped businesses captured the contract. Those Troy-bilts were made like farm tractors, though, definitely high-quality. Some of those we sold are still in use forty years later.

During those forty years we have heard some amusing stories having to do with people and their Troy-bilts. Henri has one of the best, concerning a neighbour of his, Donald, an old war veteran. Donald has passed on now and couldn't take the tiller with him. I don't know what became of it. Anyway, it seems that one summer day, Donald was working with the tiller high on a hill when black clouds and lightning swept down on him. Before he could take cover, a lightning bolt struck, knocking Donald and the tiller head over heels. Picking himself up, Donald examined the tiller and found it okay (you can't bust a Troy-bilt). Examining himself, he couldn't find anything wrong either.

The true impact of the strike didn't show up until later. It seems that, in the war, Donald had acquired a very stubborn bladder infection that he had been treating ever since—52 years. Well, that day, up on the hill with the tiller we sold him, struck by lightning, miraculously unhurt, he was cured of his bladder infection.

After giving up the rototiller, we tried selling common garden tools such as shovels and rakes, but couldn't compete. Larger outlets sold them much more cheaply. We did, however corner the market on Felco pruners, which were made in Switzerland and were the only pruners worth buying if you were a serious gardener.

Henri and Phyllis sometimes travelled in the off season to visit garden centres in other parts of North America and Europe. They brought back new ideas to try. We had some success with plant and nature books, bird houses and feeders. Organic pest control products really took off. Beneficial insects and ice cream cones never quite made it.

One success was garden statuary and large enamelled pots in bright colours for outdoor planting. Phyllis found a supplier of tasteful, enamelled-concrete statuary, such as Buddhas and sundials and Japanese lanterns, and brought in stacks of enamelled pots and planters wrapped in newspapers from Thailand or the Philippines. These were nice when planted with colourful annuals, and were large enough that plants could grow in them all summer. They proved very popular with customers and also dressed up the garden centre when we massed them outside for sale or distributed them among the plants.

Fall bulbs were a big seller in the store and also marked the change of season at the garden centre. You knew it was Fall when you came back from landscaping and smelled the fritillaria bulbs—a little like skunk. One of my landscaping buddies hid a squashed one under the seat of my truck. It was weeks before I figured out what was the stink.

Most of the bulbs, of course, were tulips and narcissus and crocus and didn't have much of a smell. Together, though, crates and crates of them in the small store, they did have a distinctive smell that meant Fall and still makes me nostalgic when I smell it at other places.

We also sold what were termed "Spring bulbs", which were planted in Spring and bloomed later in the Summer. These included lilies, gladiolus, dahlias and other less common species, and the bulb company usually tucked in a few bulbs we had never seen before. Some of these proved popular—such as acidanthera and freesia—and sold well.

One year they sent us the Voodoo plant. This mysterious bulb produced a sprawling plant with a curious waxy purple flower that smelled like rotten meat. Flies pollinated it, and it was covered with them. We had to carry it out of the greenhouse on a shovel, and it didn't sell well at all. Some supplier had a sense of humour.

The Spring bulbs came mostly in one shipment each year, from Holland. Bulbs arrived in Halifax on a container ship, and went out to garden centres across the Maritimes. One year we can't forget, a container slid off the ship in a storm and our bulbs were lost. Phyllis scrambled to find other sources and we did have bulbs—a little late.

Tropical houseplants were never a real big thing at Pleasant Valley Nurseries, but we always had some to sell to homeowners and businesses. One year, somewhere around the end of November or early December, Phyllis brought in a big order of tropical plants commissioned to be planted inside the Mall in Port Hawkesbury. Everyone at PVN had already disappeared for the winter except Henri, Phyllis and me. Phyllis and I each had a car, and Henri had a little quarter-ton truck. We left Antigonish in the morning with three vehicles jammed with plants, and ran smack into a raging blizzard.

By the time we got to Port Hawkesbury our wipers couldn't clear the windshields. Creeping towards the Mall in single file, half blinded by the snow, somehow I got a flat tire. While Phyllis and Henri kept on to the Mall to unload, I jacked up the wheel and took it off, all the while hoping no one would run me over. Henri came back for me and, since I had no spare, we spent the next hour buying a new tire and putting it back on the car.

By the time we got to the Mall and unloaded my car, there were no shoppers left inside. Store workers were all standing by the glass doors looking out at the storm and wondering if they would make it home. Shortly after that, the Mall decided to close for the day. Everyone locked up and took off immediately except for Henri, Phyllis and me.

It was dark inside except for dim emergency lights and weak light from the skylights. It was oddly quiet with the place deserted. We couldn't see outside and had no idea if the storm was still blowing or not.

We worked for hours to get all the planters done and by the time we left the Mall it was almost dark. Our cars were gone—buried in the snow. We determined that Henri's truck would be the easiest to dig out, and once it was clear we all three got in and left the other two cars where they were. The passenger door latch was frozen and once we got it open, it wouldn't close.

Somehow, we made it back to Antigonish and home. All the way I had to hold that door closed so we wouldn't slide out. The next day, once the roads were cleared, Phyllis and I went back for our cars.

One more blizzard story like any Nova Scotian can tell, with tropical plants thrown in for fun.

Just about the most anticipated event at the garden centre each Spring was the return of Henri from Ontario with a tractor-trailer load of plants. The business wasn't really ready to go until the truck arrived, and Henri went up for a few days each April to make sure it was loaded and on its way.

Unloading was a day-long job, and the entire staff pitched in, along with any friends or curious hangers-on who might be available. Unless you are enamoured of plants like we were, it is hard to describe the excitement and festive atmosphere of this day—working all together for the first time in Spring and unpacking the trailer to see what was new.

There were evergreens in pots, from tiny dwarfs to big spruces and pines that required two or three men to lift. Also there were the broadleaf evergreens—rhododendrons, hollies, azaleas and other species. Some flowering shrubs came in pots; others came leafless and with bare roots, tied up in bundles of five or ten and waiting to be potted. Fruit trees and bushes were bare-root in bundles. Some shade trees came potted, others bare root.

Everything that came bare-root had to be temporarily planted or "heeled in" into a sawdust pile to keep the roots moist until they were potted. Eventually Henri built a cold storage where trees and shrubs could be kept dormant and leafless, with the roots wetted down daily with the hose. This gave us a little more time to get on top of things in the Spring.

We could sell some of the plants straight out of the cold storage and not have to pot them at all. The rest we could pot up when we were caught up. Sometimes this wasn't until nearly July. Plants were happy in the dark and the cold as long as they didn't get bone dry. They figured it was still winter. Once they were finally potted up and set outside, they leafed out in a hurry and quickly made up for lost time.

Towards the end of unloading day, the truck always seemed empty—the big stuff was out—but there were still hundreds of small plants in one-gallon pots. These didn't take up much room and didn't look like much, but took a long time to unload. It was a long walk to the back of the trailer.

The small pots, though, were often the most interesting part of the load. Many were new species and varieties we hadn't seen before and were eager to try. Because they were small, they weren't too expensive and we could plant some of them at home. It was always a struggle at Pleasant Valley Nurseries to not spend your paycheque on plants.

A good part of the expense of bringing plants in from Ontario to Nova Scotia was, of course, the trucking. If we left it up to the nurseries in Ontario to load the truck, they would send two. This doubled the cost of trucking. Henri was sure that if the truck was loaded properly, everything would fit in one truck. This meant, however, that there was no other choice than to supervise the packing himself, so, in April, off he went to Ontario.

Henri is not one to stand by and watch others work. To their amusement, he pitched in right alongside the Sikhs and Jamaicans, and everything did indeed fit in one truck. The first few years,

Henri rode back to Antigonish with the truck driver. Though he gained a healthy respect for the trials and tribulations of truck driving, he didn't keep that up.

The trip in April to load the truck became an annual thing—one that Henri would tell you he did not look forward to. He did what he had to do, though, and came back with good stories.

In later years, Henri normally flew back and forth to Ontario, but one year I went with him in the car. In Ontario, in between loading, we took a drive down past the tobacco fields of Tillsonburg and the tomato fields of Aylmer to Point Pelee National Park, the southernmost point in Canada.

An ancient honey locust at Point Pelee.

At Point Pelee, we took a walk down the last spit of sand jutting out into Lake Erie to find out what was the final and most southerly tree in Canada. It was a white ash, if you are curious.

Also at Point Pelee, we came across a huge and ancient honey locust tree spreading wide and low in the sand dunes, with thorns four inches long and hard as iron. It looked like something from the plains of Africa. We were selling little honey locust trees in the garden centre with no idea that they grew like that in their native habitat.

The plant truck from Ontario was the most fun, but not the only truck to unload, by any means. Almost every day during the early Spring and Summer, transports and delivery trucks rolled in to be unloaded. They carried all sorts of supplies and products for us to sell at the garden centre. For years, before Henri bought his tractor, we unloaded everything by hand, piece by piece.

The worst were trucks full of peat moss or fertilizer. Peat moss came in a closed trailer packed from front to back with heavy bales. They were packed so tightly that it took two or three men to get the first one out. After that, we carried each heavy bale on our shoulder to the stack. When the trailer began to empty, two men had to drag bales the length of the truck and pass them to the stackers.

The women working at PVN became stackers, too. No one got out of it. Unloading peat moss was a big, heavy job.

Limestone, fertilizer and manure came in smaller bags and were sometimes stacked on pallets. We had no machine to unload pallets, however, so we unpacked them and carried bags one or two at a time. Good thing we were young.

When we got older, Henri finally bought a tractor that could unload full pallets and drive them to where they were to go. Eventually, even peat moss came on pallets. To make things easier for us aging baby-boomers, fertilizer companies have been putting their products in smaller and smaller bags. When Henri's father was young, fertilizer came in 40-kilogram bags—almost one hundred pounds. Now a big bag is 25 kilograms, and most are lighter than that. We may be taller than our fathers but couldn't be any tougher.

May and June at the garden centre were the money-making months. For the staff it was a hard grind, passing from one customer straight to the next. Besides wrapping up trees for customers so they didn't lose all their leaves on the way home, the hardest work at the garden centre was answering questions. Looking back, it is clear that this was the essence of the work. It was a rare customer who came in and bought something without asking questions. A sale nearly always involved a discussion eventually leading, we hoped, to the selection of the best plant or product for the situation.

These discussions—or maybe conversations would be a better word—were part of the job. It was enjoyable to meet and chat with people and to consider their questions or requests. Thinking was the hard part. No two customers ever asked exactly the same thing, and most questions required hard thinking, including formulating pertinent questions of our own to help with the decision. Getting home at night, the head was as tired as the back.

Bearing the brunt of this strenuous mental labour cheerfully, with never a frown, were the women who worked the cash at the front counter. They were generally the first ones to talk to a customer, and, nine times out of ten, answer their question. The women also answered the phone. Certain callers chose to snub the girl on the phone and ask to talk to one of the "men"—usually meaning Henri—who, to get even, would ask them to hold on while he checked with one of the women.

Janette Fecteau and Jeanette Lynes at a PVN poetry reading.

The girl at the front counter became, in a way, the heart and soul of the garden centre. Her good cheer and thoughtful advice were what kept people coming back. All the women shared time at the front counter. Yvonne, Beverley, Holly and Phyllis, and also Mary, were back and forth at the cash but had other responsibilities in the office or greenhouses, however, and couldn't be there all the time.

Men working inside the store were not unheard of, but nearly as scarce as a blue tulip. However, Garth Lowther, Tony Tomlik, and Dave Coyle all spent time up front, and even the landscapers sometimes sold plants. Students and summer help might be trained to ring in purchases, but there was always one woman who took on the front counter as her responsibility and was, at least for a time, the face of Pleasant Valley Nurseries.

The first, and probably most unforgettable—for staff and customers alike—was Linda Petite. A dynamic, curly-headed plant lover from Cape Breton, Linda did it all: yard work, greenhouse work—but she was at her best with customers. It was impossible not to smile when talking to Linda. She would very quickly help find just what you were looking for and meet you at the cash. Many customers, upon getting out of their cars, would immediately scan the place until they found Linda. No one else would do. She was lots of fun and a gardening expert. She started at the garden centre as a very young woman and worked there for many years. Today she is head gardener at the Horticultural Centre of the Pacific in Victoria, British Columbia.

When Linda moved away, we thought it was the end. We couldn't see how we could replace her. To our amazement and delight, though, Amy Van den Hoogen moved quickly into the void. Amy, a young woman from Arisaig, north of Antigonish, grew up on a dairy farm and was resourceful as farm girls are.

She wasn't Linda, which didn't matter. She brought her own personality to the job. Amy could talk to anyone and kept things moving at the cash. She started a Facebook page for the business, and was very artistic. Beautifully done signs and signboards done in chalk began to appear everywhere.

When she wasn't helping customers, Amy would round up all the plants that were blooming and looking good to make eye-popping arrangements in front of the store. These arrangements included statuary and fancy pots. They were so lovely that customers sometimes didn't realize that the plants were for sale. We had to stick price signs in everything, which spoiled the composition a little.

Amy held the fort for a few years, then suffered the same fate as many good-looking young women at the garden centre. She got married. Soon she moved on and left us wondering if we could ever replace *her*.

Aleisha Laureijs was next to the rescue. Aleisha was a no-nonsense young woman who took off alone in a car to get back to her native Antigonish after finishing school in Iowa. She was also no-nonsense at the cash and front counter, and the customers trusted her. She had no problem advising them and figuring out their problems. Garden problems, too. Aleisha was very artistic also and good at making signs and was at the garden centre for several years. We were sad when she left for more schooling, but were starting to get used to these losses.

After Aleisha came Laura Besaw and Holly's daughter, Hanna. Laura grew up near Antigonish but had spent time on a homestead in Quebec. She was a natural gardener and gave good advice at the counter. Laura was also perfectly bilingual. French-speaking customers were flattered that she could help them in their own language.

Hannah Chisholm, Holly's daughter, was a marvel. She must have had it in her genes. Both her mother and her father were expert gardeners and landscapers and it had to come out somewhere. Hannah was studying business at St. Francis Xavier University, where she spent her spare time helping set up a greenhouse to grow food for hungry students. As soon as classes were out for the year, she came to work for us. Besides helping her mother with the yard and greenhouse work, she planted a beautiful cut-flower garden by the rustic fence on the premises each year. She also put in her time at the front counter and cash, where she rang in sales and answered questions. Alas, Hannah finished school and Laura bought a place on the South Shore. They both moved on, and it was Sarah's turn.

Sarah Lancaster could, I believe, have worked anywhere. We were lucky to get her. She was the fastest learner I ever saw. She had a keen interest in plants but was starting nearly at zero. Within one or two years she had mastered all the plants, including their Latin names. She could almost always be found at the front counter or in the yard taking pictures of anything blooming for the Facebook page. Sarah was also lots of help to Phyllis in the office, keeping track of orders and inventory. She was with us all the way to the closing sale. Now she has another job. I'm not sure what she'll do with her Latin.

Phyllis was always at the counter when you needed her, and handled the messiest and most complicated questions. Also, she knew everyone and everyone knew her. Having vast amounts of paperwork to do in the office, she couldn't always be at the cash; but when she was, everyone was happy. No more wondering what to charge for the pot without a price tag on it. Customers, too, were happy to see her there. Not exactly the face of Pleasant Valley Nurseries because she was too often in the office, but certainly the heart and soul.

The garden centre at Pleasant Valley Nurseries opened each Spring by the middle of March and things picked up steadily heading into May. March and April were a time of bringing out plants from winter storage, unloading trucks of new stock and supplies, fixing up winter damage, moving in seedlings from the greenhouses in Lakevale, and generally getting ready to go. Often in April we were still shovelling snow to make way for plants, and hacking away at frozen ground. By mid-April or May, conditions had eased up a little and customers couldn't wait any longer. Cars began to fill the parking lot—gardeners coming to get their seeds and potting soil and to ask how soon we would have tomato plants, or how to put in a lawn.

Our first visitors were invariably the vegetable gardeners. In fact, almost all gardeners are vegetable gardeners first thing in

Spring. That is the time to get seeds started and put tomato plants on the windowsill. The trees and shrubs, the flowers and the lawn can wait until the ground thaws out. Very few people in this rural area of Nova Scotia don't grow something to eat. We had seed racks in the store from five or six different seed companies, with new introductions every year. We sold probably a dozen varieties of certified potato seed from P.E.I. We offered asparagus roots, strawberry plants, raspberry canes, rhubarb roots, Jerusalem artichokes, horseradish and anything else customers were asking for.

Vegetable seed and transplants and small fruit sales were a large part of our business and, in a way, the dearest to our hearts. We were all vegetable gardeners at Pleasant Valley Nurseries. In fact, that is why most of us came looking for work in the first place. PVN looked like the ideal way to work and garden at the same time. Vegetable gardening is endlessly interesting and rewarding, and none of us ever tired of it. At coffee break, nine times out of ten, if we weren't talking about Bruce Davidson, we were talking about our gardens.

In the store, and out in the yard, we talked to customers about theirs. We sold them seeds and transplants and talked about timing and cultural tips and what could take frost and what couldn't. We talked about fertilizers and preparing the soil and the safest techniques of pest control. This included control of marauding animals that could mess up the garden. My neighbour said that one time there was some animal digging up her transplants as fast as she could put them in. She called PVN, and whoever was on the phone guessed that it was a skunk or a raccoon and asked if there was a male in the house. If so, they said, have him urinate in the beds. That fixed it.

Because we were avidly growing our own vegetables and fruit, we were able to offer advice from experience, both the sweet and the bitter. Though we had lots to say, we were careful not to make it complicated or intimidating. The last thing we wanted to do was discourage anyone. Planting a garden is, in truth, such a very simple thing that a child can do it.

People—sometimes children—often approached us, excited and wanting to plant their first garden. We instructed them to select a spot in the sun, and how to prepare the soil. We helped them pick out seeds and that was basically all they needed to know. In a sunny spot, with soil that is loose and fertile, most of what you plant will surely grow, and another gardener is born. Gardening after that is just a question of experience and fine tuning.

At Pleasant Valley Nurseries we also had the privilege of meeting many long-time gardeners—often more experienced than ourselves. We learned as much from them as they did from us, and we passed what we learned to others.

Starting in May, and all the way through June we were open 11 hours a day, 7 days a week. As the weather warmed people began to think of trees and shrubs, and had their lawns raked out ready for fertilizer and seed. Phyllis had the entrance to the store full of trays of pansies and violets she had started for gardeners who couldn't wait.

By mid-June there was little danger of frost and we could finally open the greenhouses and sell everything. By then people were all coming at once and we were just about run off our feet. Some days our parking lot looked like the one at Canadian Tire. We called May and June the busy season. Ask anyone who ever worked at Pleasant Valley Nurseries about the busy season, and they'll know just what you mean.

Our year was basically two months. By Canada Day, July 1, gardeners had their planting finished and were at the beach with the kids. At the garden centre sales began to slow and we were back to the eight-hour day. The cash register had a chance to cool down and the staff had a party to celebrate surviving another busy season.

The end of the busy season meant a rest for the workers, but also an uncomfortably long stretch of low revenues ahead. We spent a great deal of time over the years trying to figure out how to make the busy season longer—a ghastly idea that proved to be impossible. There were ways, however, to make the busy season busier, and we couldn't argue with that.

Advertising was something Henri and Phyllis took seriously. For the first decade or so of Pleasant Valley Nurseries, Henri put in a great deal of work and spent most of his winter designing catalogues to distribute at the store and through the mail. The catalogues were illustrated and included concise descriptions of all the plants we had to sell, as well as gardening tips and information. We were all quite proud of the catalogues and excited to pass them out.

In conjunction with the catalogue, Henri and Phyllis worked with artist Stefan Gerriets to create newspaper ads, mostly published in the Antigonish *Casket*, for their products, services and weekly specials. They also placed ads with CJFX radio. For a while, Henri even hosted a weekly gardening show on CJFX with Gus MacKinnon. This, coupled with the catalogue and the advertising, certainly brought more business to PVN, and made the busy season busier.

Advertising also helped spread sales out more evenly, as we could promote specials throughout the Summer and Fall.

Mother's and Father's Days took place during the busy season and were a boon to garden centres. We spruced up the displays and advertised to make the most of these days—lilies and roses and maybe a rhododendron for Mom and a tree for Dad. We would have welcomed Son and Daughter and First Cousin days, too.

Eventually we employed the Internet to further our fortunes, from a comprehensive early website that Ian Bryon designed and Henri's son Jason later re-tooled, to Amy's and Sarah's Facebook page. Pleasant Valley Nurseries also hosted a low-key photography contest with gardening prizes. Customers came in with their nicest photos of their properties and gardens, which were interesting and truly beautiful.

Henri and Phyllis hosted gardening workshops and poetry readings to bring people into the garden centre, and there was a not-too successful attempt to sell ice cream and coffee from a rustic little building we called the "Bumblebee Cafe", which, incidentally, has since been donated to the Keppoch recreation area.

Each of us was asked from time to time to talk to garden clubs and societies, to judge displays at the Fall exhibition, or to plant a commemorative tree for some occasion, and were happy to comply after first trying to get Henri to do it. But, seriously, we all knew that any publicity we got would help the business to "bumble" along.

A milestone at Pleasant Valley Nurseries each year, and a final heroic push to sell everything we could, was the annual "Fall sale". This sale started after Labour Day and was timed to coincide with cooler and damper Autumn weather and to promote the "second" planting season. At this time of year planting conditions were again ideal. Trees and shrubs were going dormant for the winter and losing their leaves, but the soil was still warm enough that, if they were planted, they would grow roots before freeze-up. Also, kids were back in school and parents had more time. In Fall the maples in the woods were unbelievable and the weather was perfect for working. Also, we marked everything down drastically at the garden centre.

Several weeks of work were necessary to get ready for the Fall sale. We had to cross out and change prices on each of the hundreds of signs throughout the yard. An inventory was necessary to determine what plants we had left and how many of each. The sale price might be 10% to 50% off, and depended upon how many of that plant we had left. The discount was greatest on varieties that we had most of.

Customers soon caught on that they could save significantly if they waited until Fall to buy plants. Some of them started scouting out the garden centre a couple of weeks before the sale to plan what they would snap up on the first day. We were fine with that. After all, what we had by then were the leftovers and we were eager to sell them. The best plants had usually been purchased through the Spring and Summer at full price by gardeners who didn't want to gamble. That isn't to say you couldn't find great plants at Pleasant Valley Nurseries in the Fall. What we had left over, though, tended to be lesser known and lesser appreciated varieties, and things we had too many of anyway.

Consequently, the Fall sale was as good for us as it was for gardeners. The sale brought in a flurry of business that was welcome after the slow dog-days of Summer. Customers saved money and we were able to move a significant quantity of plant material that we would otherwise have had to store and care for through the winter. Also, though we were extremely careful not to sell a plant that had anything wrong with it, we were relieved, in the Fall, not to have to deal with a guarantee.

Nothing at Pleasant Valley Nurseries caused so much confusion as the guarantee. Customers, understandably, expected some sort of guarantee on the trees and shrubs they purchased. Often plants were purchased in early Spring before leaves came out and they could be pretty dead-looking. Customers were justifiably suspicious and reluctant to fork out money without a guarantee.

The trouble is, we were selling living creatures. The customer had every right to demand that his or her plant be in good health when purchased, and we had no problem with that. The difficulty was that there were a lot of things that could kill a healthy plant once it left the yard. Replacing plants that died for no fault of our own was hard to accept and hard on the business. The infrequent upsetting altercations with a customer at PVN usually involved a debate over whether a plant was bad when we sold it and should be replaced, or went bad after leaving the premises.

We had to offer a guarantee period long enough that there could be no question that the tree or shrub was healthy when taken home. I had just been to the pet shop—which also sells living things—to buy a guinea pig with my daughter. They also have to guarantee what they sell. They gave us a week. Customers at PVN, though, expected more than a week. In fact, they told us that our competitors were offering a year. Our competitors, however, also sold groceries, or hardware, or building supplies and could afford to lose a little money on trees. Still, we decided to capitulate-- our first guarantee was for a year.

This did not work out well. When Spring came, it sometimes seemed that every second person in the garden centre had a dead tree in a bag. We couldn't prove that the tree wasn't dead before it was run over by the car, pulled up by the dog, gnawed by mice, or hit by the snowplow, so we replaced it. Most dead trees were dead from drowning in wet ground. They had done well all summer while conditions were dry, but died in waterlogged ground as the snow melted the following Spring. Again, this was hard to prove, so we replaced a lot of trees.

We realized that we couldn't afford to guarantee trees over winter again and settled on a guarantee to October 1st. This met with skepticism at first, but proved in the end to afford a reasonable period of time to evaluate the plant.

By the way, the guinea pig had fleas. but we treated them at home and didn't take him back.

Another realization was that we must insist that people keep the receipt for the tree or shrub they had purchased. We had discovered that it happened that people brought back dead plants purchased elsewhere, expecting a replacement. I believe they really thought that they had purchased the plant from us, but memory is a funny thing. Also, without a receipt we had no idea whether we had sold the plant at regular price, or on a special. A receipt would have settled everything. We pleaded with customers to keep their slips, and of course, everyone promised they would, and meant it. Most shrubs and trees were bought and planted in May or June and guaranteed until October. By October, those slips could be anywhere. We knew most of our customers and often remembered what they had bought.

We were trapped. It was tough to face up to a loyal customer and refuse to replace their plant just because they had lost the receipt. Usually we caved in, then were on the wrong side of customers who had been refused. We had to learn to treat everyone the same, like every other business did, and customers had to learn that we were a business, too. Eventually we did and they did. Also, homeowners were becoming much better gardeners and there were not as many dead plants coming back.

Curious customers, who observed that we still had a lot of stock left after the Fall sale, frequently asked us what we were going to do with it all. They were often surprised that most of it could be left outdoors in protected areas of the yard. After all, almost everything was hardy for our winters and wouldn't likely be damaged by the cold.

We did have unheated greenhouses in the lower part of the yard that we covered in white plastic and used to store evergreens, perennials and woody plants such as magnolias and Japanese maples that were borderline hardy. The white covering was intended to reflect the sun and keep the building cold inside. The objective was to give the plants a bit of shelter from the elements but keep them dormant. If the house warmed up too much on a sunny day, the plants inside would begin to grow and be killed when the temperature plunged at night.

Moving plants into their winter storage was a big job after the garden centre closed in November. Even though we sold a lot of plants during the Fall sale, there were always enough left over to make for a couple of weeks' work. We had to clean up and cut back thousands of perennials, then move them tray by tray down to storage at the bottom of the drive. Holly and Beverly did most of this. I disliked helping with the perennials because of all the awkward stooping to pick up heavy trays off the ground. Sometimes it doesn't pay to be six feet tall.

Perennials went into one of the storage greenhouses and evergreens and tender shrubs and trees into the other. We picked up all the hardy shrubs and crowded them together in the upper end of the yard with sawdust packed around the pots for insulation. We moved leftover trees to the same area, lined them up together and, and nestled them deeply enough into the sawdust that they shouldn't blow over. Trees were heavy and no fun to move. They were the last thing we put away. By then the snow was starting to fly.

Snug for the winter.

The spot at the top of the yard where we nestled or "heeled" in the trees and shrubs was sheltered from the sun and the wind by the fertilizer barn on one side and hedges and shrubbery on the others. Neither wind nor sun could damage trees here over the winter. The sawdust covering the pots protected vulnerable roots from the cold.

The only things left to worry about were snow breakage and mice. Both hit us hard more than once. In a winter of heavy snow, the fact that the area was sheltered would cause the snow to accumulate. If it froze to the trees it could tear the branches right off when it sank in a thaw. Just the weight of a heavy snowfall could break branches. Underneath the snow, mice worked invisibly to gnaw bark. Even if trees were not killed, they might as well have been. A tree with broken branches or mouse damage was a tree that we couldn't sell.

Nevertheless, if we watched the snow buildup and took care of mice, trees came out of this area in good shape in the Spring. It had taken us a few years to work out this seemingly simple routine. The first year Henri had trees at the new garden centre, he decided to leave them where they were, planted out in a field next to the highway. After all, they were hardy, their roots were in the ground, and after a year in the row they were solidly rooted and couldn't blow over. Leaving them in place saved us a lot of work.

The catch was that the highway was the Trans-Canada, and traffic alongside the garden centre was heavy and fast. The road was copiously salted to melt the snow. Passing trucks and fast traffic stirred up the salty water and slush, and the Northwest wind whipped it across the field to coat the trees. All were damaged or killed that winter as this coating of salt wicked out moisture from the bark and the buds. We hadn't seen it coming.

Next year we overcompensated by deciding to dig up all the trees and truck them into the barn in Pleasant Valley. This was a gruelling job and I remember it vividly. I really shouldn't have been helping that Fall because it was getting late and I was supposed to start my second year at the Agriculture College. My wife and kids were already in Truro, but I was camped out at the store in Antigonish, sleeping on bags of lawn seed.

Henri and I and a young student named Jeff van Zwol were working overtime to get the job finished. The other men had already quit for the season. This is when Henri decides to sprain his ankle, and I mean really sprain it—almost broken. He jumped off the back of the ton truck straight onto a round piece of firewood that turned his ankle under. All his weight came down on it. End of the season for Henri—he was on crutches. Jeff and I would have to finish the work alone. I gave up trying to get back to Truro in time for classes—I was already late.

We managed to finish late in November, in the dark, driving our last load of trees to the barn in a raging blizzard with no idea if we would get home. Evidently we did, and I'll always be grateful to Jeff for his steadfast and uncomplaining work. Jeff worked with us for quite a few summers after that until he finished University and left to get a real job.

So that was it for the season. Plants all put away, storage houses closed up securely, the store a mess inside but that could wait until Spring, chain pulled across the drive, and a wave to Willie and we were gone. Henri claims that it was only because the garden centre closed during the winter that he stayed sane.

To celebrate one more season at Pleasant Valley Nurseries come and gone, Henri and Phyllis, our good employers, took the entire staff to a nice restaurant and paid the bill—including drinks. How could we not return in the Spring?

What we had going for us

Pleasant Valley Nurseries was a long shot. How was it that a small tree nursery and garden centre in this out-of-the-way corner of Northeastern Nova Scotia could survive—let alone become one of the best in Canada? Even Henri admits that he couldn't have picked a more unlikely place to start a nursery.

By and large, the good soil in Nova Scotia has run out by the time you get to Antigonish County. Pictou County next door has good agricultural soil, and so do parts of Cape Breton. Not so in Antigonish County. Soils tend to be heavy, poorly drained, stony and thin. Any good agricultural soil here has been occupied for generations, and isn't for sale to twenty-year-olds. Henri had his choice of worked-out marginal farms for his nursery, and settled for one.

The hardiness zone on this farm was as marginal as the soil. Hardiness zones give an indication of where a particular species of plant can grow without freezing to death. The lower the number, the colder the zone. Antigonish County lies in zones 5a and 5b—not quite zone 6. Zone 6 is slightly warmer in the winter and all the good stuff grows in zone 6. All the exotics that Henri struggled to grow in Lakevale would have been easy in zone 6.

Henri wouldn't have had to travel very far to set up his nursery in zone 6. He also wouldn't have had to travel far to find better soil. Travelling anywhere, though was out of the question. Henri was determined to stay in Antigonish, and that was that. The rest of us are thankful that he did.

The story of Pleasant Valley Nurseries might be likened to a remarkable conjunction of the stars—a fortuitous alignment of youthful enthusiasm and naiveté, the influx of back-to-the-landers into Antigonish County in the 70s, the horticulture program at the A.C., the explosion of interest in gardening, the garden clubs and garden societies, the increasingly sophisticated gardeners, the cresting wave of baby boomers, and Henri's dream.

That this story takes place in Antigonish is no accident. Those of us playing leading roles came to Antigonish in a variety of ways, but liked what we found here and were determined to stay. It was a time when idealistic youth could choose where they wanted to live, then how to make a living.

Youth, in the 1970s, were surprisingly eager to get back to the land. This was especially unsettling for their parents who had grown up on hardscrabble farms and escaped. After World War II they had found good-paying jobs in the cities and given their children the best of everything. Now the darn kids wanted to go back to those worn-out farms and live off the land. Well, let them find out.

Antigonish County, in the 70s, had a lot of worn-out farms and cut-over woodland, and it didn't cost much to buy a few acres. Henri had his farm house and 12 acres in Pleasant Valley. He was beginning to plant seeds and start his little nursery. On other old farms and pieces of land, young people were building homesteads and planting gardens. They looked for advice from experienced local neighbours and their enthusiasm even got the old folks going. Interest in gardening was on the rise. It was a good time to start a nursery business.

The wave of children born after World War II was coming of age —the baby boom. In their earliest and most outrageous incarnation, baby boomers were the hippies. They were also the homesteaders and back-to-the-landers settling in Antigonish County. They were the flower children. Baby boomers were educated, thanks to their parents, and mostly undamaged by war or depression. They were in favour of nature and growing things.

By their sheer numbers they influenced towns and governments to plant, bringing PVN much needed work. As they grew older and their children were leaving home, many turned to gardening with enthusiasm, joining garden clubs and plant societies and spending money cheerfully on plants and supplies. It was this swelling wave of committed gardeners that we turned to, after giving up landscaping in 2000, to carry us forward. This they did, and we were relieved to find that there was life after landscaping. We turned our full attention to focus on the advantages we had.

By this time, everyone was selling plants. Building supplies, hardware stores, grocery stores and even gas stations sold nursery stock trucked in from far away. Walmart and Superstore were coming to town. To them, I guess this looked like an easy way to make some money. They must have seen the traffic jams in the parking lot at Pleasant Valley Nurseries in May and June.

Unfortunately, they were slow to learn that plants are living creatures and have to be looked after. Some of the stock they were selling was the same as what we sold. It looked pretty good when it came in, but, as a rule, went downhill fast. Garden centre help who knew anything about plants and would work for minimum wage were scarce. Consequently, their strategy was to sell the plants quickly and cheaply while they still looked good. By August they were clearing out the leftovers for any price they could get. I saw one place selling dead plants for half price.

They may have been beating us on prices but we were beating them on everything else. Our plant selection was better beyond comparison and the plants were looked after and healthy. Our buildings and grounds were attractive—a far cry from their cold-frame greenhouses hastily thrown up in the parking lot. Our best asset of all was the people we saw daily—on both sides of the cash register. On our side were committed and educated plant people. We weren't building-supply salesmen or grocery-store clerks or service-station attendants pressed into service selling plants. We were avid gardeners and plant lovers in our own right, and many of us were trained at the Nova Scotia Agriculture College in Truro.

Working at Pleasant Valley Nurseries, however, quickly taught us A.C. graduates that we still had plenty to learn. As in any profession, a degree from school is only the beginning. In educational terms, one day at the garden centre during the madness of June was worth ten at the Agriculture College. More than one who put their shoulder to the wheel at PVN came with no formal horticulture experience, and learned their plants the hard way. The "hard way" meant being bombarded with questions and requests for advice during the Spring rush.

We worked as a team, though, and those with experience helped the others. Horticulture school was a big help, though anyone smart and interested in plants could learn by working. Just ask Rose or Janette, Mary Penny, Julia, Amy Buckland-Nicks, Laura, Hannah, Chantal, Kim or Sarah, among others, who liked the work and quickly settled in.

A handful of us made careers at Pleasant Valley Nurseries and, along with Henri and Phyllis, came back year after year to keep things together. Regular customers will always remember Linda Petite, whose enthusiasm and love of plants were contagious, and who worked at PVN for years. Beverly Fraser and Holly Chisholm were indispensable and were there to the end. All three worked where they were needed, helping customers and planting up all the beautiful hanging baskets and planters that PVN was known for. Beverly was in charge of the town planters, which took up almost an entire greenhouse. Holly also worked in the greenhouses, but was found most often working with the perennials. No one knew perennials like Holly and we depended on her to keep them straight. Mary Partridge drew the landscape plans, which were something no other business in our area could offer. Out in the yard, I was the "tall guy" and worked with the trees and shrubs, and the planting crew.

Most of the men at Pleasant Valley Nurseries worked with the landscape crew. This was another sure way to learn horticulture. Landscaping was an opportunity to try the plants we sold at the garden centre, and find out how they did in the real world. We learned about soils by digging into them. As we travelled around, we discovered plants we weren't familiar with and combinations that did or did not go well together. We knew where the tulip tree was in Port Hawkesbury, and the copper beech in Boylston. This was all valuable stuff when it came time to decide what to recommend and what to sell at the garden centre.

Our employers, Henri and Phyllis, were of course co-captains and leaders of the team. Without them there would have been no business. Theirs was the job of directing PVN through all the twists and turns it took over the years—deciding what was profitable and what we could do to keep it attractive to customers.

On top of working alongside their employees, they ordered from suppliers, dealt with the banks, arranged advertising in the newspapers and on the radio, figured out sales and promotions, took care of the payroll, and worried about the bottom line while the rest of us were asleep. They took care of problems and complaints and customers who wouldn't pay their bill. Above all they were friends to their employees and lost sleep if one was unhappy. Staff tended to stick with them for decades, and we are dear friends today.

Everyone at PVN, out of necessity, became adept at fixing the regular run of breakdowns—broken water lines, torn plastic, washouts, trees blown over and the like. The place was really held together, though, by a series of incredibly talented and inventive tradesmen who looked after major repairs to the buildings, and improvements as the business grew. In the early days, Mike Joyce built staircases, shelves and railings to dress up the garden centre. Grady Poe supervised construction of the fertilizer barn and outbuildings in town, as well as Henri and Phyllis' house and barns in Lakevale. Bill van de Sande and Marty Alpert masterminded all the complicated electrical wiring required for the store, the cold storage, and the greenhouses, and Marty did the plumbing. Later on, Dwight How directed almost impossible renovations to the garden centre store, which had long passed its best-before date. From day one, Hughie MacFarlane and his father kept our tanks filled, our tires patched, and our tired old trucks on the road and working. These men were forever generous with their time and ideas. They were our friends, and as important to the business as the rest of us.

At Pleasant Valley Nurseries it was nice enough to be working together; but across from us, on the other side of the cash register, were our customers, and they made it all worthwhile. They, of course, paid our bills, but they also made the garden centre a lively and interesting place to be. Many gardeners who found their way to PVN were experts in their own right, and enjoyed a lively exchange. Some were members of garden clubs and plant societies. Others were just getting started in gardening and eager to learn how to begin. We always enjoyed getting a new gardener started. Then there were those who weren't particularly excited about gardening but were happy to let us pick out plants for them and design their plantings.

And, to be honest, maybe there were a few customers whom we didn't want to see driving into the yard. These people, upon entering the store, often found that the regulars—who had been inside moments before—had suddenly remembered something they had to do further down in the yard, leaving some puzzled and clueless summer student alone at the counter. This type of customer was infrequent, though, and didn't diminish the pleasure we got from all the good ones.

Customers at PVN were loyal and there were more every year. We made friends whom we looked for each Spring. More than once we spotted among our customers and friends an actual celebrity we recognized from television or the movies.

One of the earliest to visit the garden centre was the young Elizabeth May, who was fresh from her victorious campaign against the spruce budworm spray. She was our kind of people—she was one of us. At the time she was in to select plants for her parents' restaurant in Margaree Harbour, but she soon left us behind in her climb to become leader of the federal Green Party!

Television personalities Jim Nunn and Parker Barss-Donham came in from time to time, and we met Linden MacIntyre and Carol Off from the CBC. Premier Rodney MacDonald once bought a tree, and we did landscaping work for writer Charles Gaines and sculptor Richard Serra and their wives Patricia and Clara.

Because we worked alongside the Trans-Canada Highway, we were witness over the years to some impressive cavalcades of cars passing by, including two Prime Ministers and the Pope. Terry Fox passed by in the early days of his run, and Rick Hansen—the Man in Motion—wheeled by in his wheelchair.

None of them bought trees, but the foreign minister of Bhutan did—a lilac—the "Beauty of Moscow", as it were. We don't know what this particular French hybrid meant to him, but he and his aides spent some time picking it out. Lilacs were blooming in Antigonish at the time, and the foreign minister had been at a function of the Coady Institute. He smiled and assured us that he would be able to get it through customs.

The president of the farmer's union of Malawi, Abiel Banda, also visited once and we showed him around. Camaraderie with our customers, famous or not, was among the intangibles that made for happiness on both sides of the counter at our small-town garden centre in Antigonish.

Valued customers included towns, businesses and institutions hiring us to do plantings and maintain them. When Henri was just getting started, the mayor of Antigonish—Colin H. Chisholm—not only helped him set up a garden centre at the Mall, but commissioned the tree plantings on Main Street and in neighbourhoods around town. In later years the town of Antigonish, prompted by its Beautification Committee, decorated lavishly each summer with hanging baskets and planters, mostly from Pleasant Valley Nurseries. The Committee, David Miller and Aida Arnold, Dr. Minoli Amit and Dr. John Hamilton, and Ernie and Adrienne MacLaughlin, worked tirelessly and without pay to convince Town Council of the wisdom of spending money on trees and flowers, and we were the happy recipients of much of this largesse. As a result of their efforts, Antigonish is known today for the beauty of its downtown as much as for its Highland Games, and the two coincide. It has repeatedly won top awards from Communities in Bloom.

We also had a solid relationship with the towns of New Glasgow, Canso and Port Hawkesbury, each of which generously bought plants and commissioned work. In Port Hawkesbury, for a time, we did as much work as we did in Antigonish, planting street trees and ornamental beds around town. Doreen Alexander and Paula Davis deserve special thanks for promoting our company and finding us work with the town. Henri still gets phone calls from there for tree consultations.

The Antigonish Garden Club was good for Pleasant Valley Nurseries. The club was founded in 1983, just when we needed to know that there were people in Antigonish County as crazy about gardening as we were. In fact, there were many more than we realized, and the new garden club was exactly what they were waiting for. Some were our friends, and the rest became our friends. All were frequently at the garden centre and always had something to teach us. Some even bought plants, but not many. They were too darn good at growing their own. In a short time, the Antigonish Garden Club had over thirty members and was a wonderful asset to both town and county, and a boost to Pleasant Valley Nurseries.

Antigonish Garden Club fall rally.

Other garden clubs in the region were also a great support for PVN. There were flourishing garden clubs in Pictou and Guysborough counties, and into Cape Breton. Members of these clubs visited our garden centre, and we got to know them. Sometimes a whole group arrived on a tour. We were enthusiastic gardeners at Pleasant Valley Nurseries, and for an enthusiastic gardener there is no one easier to talk to than a garden clubber.

In Antigonish, Pleasant Valley Nurseries was located across from the shopping mall alongside what was always called the Trans-Canada Highway until that road was re-routed in 2012. This location had advantages that Henri was only half aware of when he bought the property. Being next to a heavily-travelled highway meant that prospective customers might spot us as they passed and drive in on a whim. For anyone coming on purpose, it made us easy to find.

To make sure we *were* easy to find, we put up a big sign with our name and logo, fastened to a wooden framework on tall wooden posts. On the bottom of the sign we attached an advertising board on which, from a ladder, we could put up messages by sliding in Plexiglas letters. The messages had to do with our special sales, holiday announcements, planting tips and things like that. We changed the messages regularly, but not every day.

Our garden centre was on the corner where Church Street crossed the Trans-Canada at the traffic lights. This was a popular place for hitch-hikers to wait for rides to Cape Breton, and often they sat on the grass at night under our sign, waiting to get picked up.

One night, apparently, rides were slow and someone shinnied up the post to our message board to have a little fun. He, or she, or they, rearranged the letters into lewd words and phrases very inappropriate for a garden centre. The worst part was that we didn't look at that board every day. Those words and phrases were up there for a few days before we noticed. There were probably hundreds of parents who had driven past holding their hands over their children's eyes. We were lucky we didn't make national TV.

We couldn't help but chuckle ourselves, and admire the audacity of whoever did it, but it had to stop. We concluded that the best thing would be to make it impossible to shinny up the post in the first place. We considered filling a moat with liquid manure, but settled for driving down-slanting nails into the posts like porcupine quills and cutting off the heads. Apparently, our joker lost some hide on these nails a few nights later and retaliated by yanking up our trees and throwing them all over the place. After that I guess we were even-Steven and had no more trouble.

Despite this incident and assorted other minor vandalism, we never doubted that our location on the Trans-Canada was a good one. We were never sure, however, until the highway was re-routed in 2012, how many customers came in just because they had seen us as they drove by. We flattered ourselves by believing that most people were coming on purpose and would find us wherever we were. Maybe the fact that we were now bypassed by the highway would make no difference.

Analysis of sales over the next couple of years proved otherwise, however. The loss of the highway drastically diminished revenue and was a major contributing factor to the closing of the business. Proof, nevertheless, that our location on the highway had been good for us while it lasted.

An incontestable advantage we had over our competitors was that we were bilingual. Well, no, not English and French—though we sometimes had someone working for us who could speak both. Rather, English and Latin—every plant has a name in Latin, and there are good reasons for that.

The Swedish botanist Carl Linnaeus, working in the middle 1700s, invented a workable system to make sense of the stupendous variety of plant material known at that time. There had to be a name that was unique and unambiguous for each plant, and that gave an indication of the relationship of that species to others. He accomplished this admirably by giving to each species a name, or rather two names, in Latin, like a first and last name. This is termed a binomial and is actually more like a last name followed by a first name.

The last name (which comes first) is the Genus, and the next name is the species. These Latin names are descriptive. The Genus name indicates the place of the particular specimen in the larger plant world, while the species name belongs to it alone. In the case of the sunflower *Helianthus annuus*, the Genus name tells us that it is a sunflower—Helianthus—and the species name tells us which one. Since there are about 70 different plants called sunflower in North America, this is the only way to know exactly which one we are talking about.

Genus names are further organized into families and so on. Knowing the Latin names of plants and using Linnaeus' system, it is possible to learn the relationship of one plant to all others. How else would we find out that our native ash trees are in the same family as, and therefore related to, the Mediterranean olive tree? Or that the apple is related to the rose?

That Carl Linnaeus was not in it for fame or fortune might be deduced by the fact that of the thousands of plants he classified and named for others, the only plant he named for himself is the twinflower (*Linnaea borealis*)—-a delicate, pink-flowered creeper found in mossy woods, including here in Nova Scotia. Incidentally, the twinflower is related to the honeysuckle.

Common names are colourful but confusing. Different plants are often known by the same name, or a certain plant might be known by several different names. What we call a larch tree is a tamarack or a hackmatack or a juniper, depending on where you live. What we call a mountain ash is a dogwood in Guysborough County. This is why at Pleasant Valley Nurseries we used the Latin names among ourselves. We alphabetized our price lists by Latin names. It was the only way to always know which plant we were talking about. We weren't just putting on airs. It's the way things are done in a real plant business.

Willie was an advantage, too. On the very corner of our corner at the intersection of Church Street with the Trans-Canada was Willie's place. Willie Westenenk lived in a small house that was part of a property he bought in 1976. Next to the house he had built a garage and a greenhouse. He had a large lawn that he kept immaculately mowed, and flower beds filled with flowers. He was a woodworker and built windmills and brightly painted cutouts of plywood good enough to get him on TV (Wayne Rostad, Arthur Black). Finished pieces included a life-size Santa and reindeer attached to the side of his house at Christmas, and a life-size nativity. Each summer he covered his lawn in plywood flamingos. He planted a near-perfect vegetable garden and gave most of it away to the food bank. Lots of people thought he was Pleasant Valley Nurseries. He wasn't, but we didn't always bother to straighten them out.

First, it was Willie who sold Henri the land to build his garden centre. At that time, Willie worked as the head of grounds maintenance at St. F. X. University, and lived in the little house with his wife

Lillian. He and Lillian had met in Nova Scotia after St. F.X. imported Willie from Holland to take care of their grounds in 1952. This was after he finished his military service with the Dutch army. Willie had worked in landscaping and nurseries in Holland and was well qualified for the job. He arrived in Nova Scotia speaking only Dutch, but he picked up English quickly.

Willie Westenenk on his 90th birthday, with Henri and Phyllis.

Willie retired from St. F.X. in November, 1992 after 40 years of service. This meant he had much more time to observe what we were doing behind his house at the garden centre. If he disapproved of anything, he could tune us up fluently in either of two languages.

Willie was generally good-natured, however, and when the garden centre was busy he was tolerant of the procession of cars kicking up the dust alongside his garden and the stacks of peat moss toppling over onto his lawn. He never could understand, though, why we didn't keep our grass mowed and trimmed and plant more flowers.

Tuning us up didn't seem to help, so Willie, who had grounds maintenance in his blood, took on the job himself—mowing grass and planting flowers for our benefit. On top of that, he kept an eye on the place at night, ran off intruders, and saved us more than once from catastrophic power outages and ruptured water lines.

Needless to say, we were grateful and Henri was happy to let him help himself in the store to any planting supplies he needed for his garden. Willie seemed to need a lot of supplies for that little garden—more like an excuse to chat up the pretty girls at the counter, I think. They loved him.

Willie was there from the day the garden centre started to the day it was torn down. He just turned 92 years old in November, 2020 and shows no signs of slowing down. The girls aren't safe yet. His place looks as good as it ever did and so does he. We owe him many thanks for all those years helping us to keep the place up, and just for being Willie

So much for the advantages of Pleasant Valley Nurseries over its rivals. There were personal advantages to those of us lucky enough to work there, and these were enormous. The stage is set by the insistent refrain of Henri Steeghs that he never wanted to be a businessman and a boss. He only wanted to grow trees and sell them and needed to start a company to do that. He was young and didn't know what he was getting into.

He did become a boss, however reluctantly—or an "employer' he would rather you said. There never was an "employer" who cared more about the happiness and satisfaction of those who worked for him. If someone was difficult or discouraged or down-in-the-dumps, Henri took it to heart and didn't sleep until things were right again. When Phyllis joined him, that's the way she was, too. They never fired anyone in the 44 years of Pleasant Valley Nurseries, always finding a way to work things out.

We had occasional staff meetings, whenever we could get everyone together at the same time, to hash out problems and suggestions. Better yet, we had coffee breaks in the back room—twice a day. Here we could laugh and joke, or talk in earnest. We could be relaxed and share our experiences and our observations and our lives. Henri says, in his opinion, the lowly coffee break was crucial to the morale of staff and the success of the business. More good ideas and good vibrations came from the coffee break than from a month of staff meetings. Twice a day coffee was the best way to keep the business purring along. We maintained a hole in the fence between us and the Co-op grocery and bought a steady supply of cinnamon buns.

PVN gang End of Season party.

Henri and Phyllis required seasonal help at the garden centre every summer. Including the regulars, the list of those who worked there at one time or another is almost unbelievable—104 by my count, and I may have missed a few. Pleasant Valley Nurseries was the fun place to work and appealed to hippies, back-to-the-landers, musicians looking for a day job, the temporarily unemployed, the permanently unemployed, students, artists, gardeners, plant lovers and dreamers of every description. We had some of each. Almost without exception, all will tell you that working at PVN was one of the best times of their lives.

For some of us, Pleasant Valley Nurseries *was* our life. There were weddings celebrated and babies born. We raised kids from babies to grown-ups and even to helping on the landscape crew and at the garden centre. We built homes and grew gardens of our own from our earnings. We became friends. There are no friends like those with whom you have worked daily for years. We shared Summer campouts at Linda Petite's cottage in Marble Mountain, and got together at each other's places in the Winter to laugh about old times.

Today, Pleasant Valley Nurseries is gone but we will always be friends, and the old times are as funny as they ever were and Henri doesn't have to be the boss anymore. If you can make a living and a life doing something you like with people like these, in a place as nice as Antigonish, count yourself one in a million.

The business was unable to carry on. Permanent staff was getting older and there was no point hiring new people. It was time to call it quits. Henri and Phyllis tried to sell the business without success. There were a few interested inquiries, but never quite the right fit.

Pleasant Valley Nurseries closed its doors on May 1, 2017. On September 17, 2018 the buildings were demolished—erased—to avoid further taxes. Henri, Phyllis, Willie and I watched incredulously, with lumps in our throats, as a couple of blows from a huge excavator smashed the little store where we spent so many years. It was a sad end and a stark demonstration of the surprising fragility of the stick buildings in which we live out our lives. Henri and Phyllis have since sold the land.

Could a Pleasant Valley Nurseries happen again? I wouldn't bet on it. The world has changed too much. Is plant identification even taught at University anymore? Do students comb the fields and forests to make their plant collections? Are they captured by the wonder and beauty of growing things while they are young? Are they intoxicated with the freedom of outdoor work and of growing and selling what they grow? Is the dream still alive in this age of the cell phone. I hope so.

Now (January, 2021) it is a year since I wrote that last comment. The pandemic has persuaded me to change my tune. With people forced to stay home, gardening has taken a huge upswing and just maybe—a PVN *will* happen again.

Bruce Partridge B.Sc., dipl. Hort., EAWC[2] Jan. 2021

Bruce and Henri, at the finish line.

---

2 Edged Around the World Club—an elite society of those landscapers who have edged a minimum of 25,000 miles (40,000 km.) of planting beds during their career. Edging is traditionally done with spade and grub hoe, but since 1985 edges done with the sod cutter are eligible. Membership is contingent upon exemplary behaviour while edging, such as not cursing audibly after accidentally cutting the customer's satellite cable or the wire to his outdoor lamp post.

Bruce Partridge

The team

Those who worked at Pleasant Valley Nurseries, 1973-2017:

Perennials

Al Benoit
Laura Besaw
Stephen Besaw
Frank Campbell
Holly Chisholm
Paul Chisholm
Hannah Chisholm
Kim Curry
Bruce Davidson
Janette Fecteau
Beverley Fraser
Dave Hoar
Stefan Gerriets
Chris Griffiths
Sarah Lancaster
Julia Legge
Garth Lowther
Aleisha Laureijs
Yvonne Maas
Jack MacLeod
Doug Myer
Susie Murphy
Rose Murphy
Bruce Partridge
Mary Partridge
Mary Penny
Linda Petite
Henri Steeghs
Phyllis Baker-Steeghs
Jason Steeghs
Aaron Steeghs
Nathan Steeghs
Pete Stovell
Tony Tomlik
Tracey Tomlik
Amy Van den Hoogen
Jeff Van Zwol
Leif Watson

Bruce Partridge

Annuals

Marty Alpert
Clem Anson
Helene Arsenault
Pam Bailey
Vincent Basque
Justine Bloomfield
Daniel Boudreau
Bill Briand
Ian Bryson
Amy Buckland-Nicks
Nukalu Callaghan-Patriachar
Mary Campbell
Ben Campbell
Rebecca Campbell
Christina Carreau
Austin Carter
Sean Chisholm
Derf Chisholm
Emily Chisholm
Lauren Chisholm
Adrian Coady
Katherine Cormier
David Coyle
Megan Cranford (MacInnis)
Jamie Ellison
Mark Fawcett-Atkinson
Will Frankland
Daniel Fraser
Sandy Forbes
Maryanne Gillis

Neil Gillis
June Good
Martha Gorman
Meghan Jackson
James Steele
Mike Joyce
Mike Kyte
Rod Landry
Gunnie Laureijs
Alexandra Lynch
Cheryl MacDonald
Kevin MacDonald
Erin MacKenzie
Catherine MacKenzie
Graham MacKenzie
Patsy MacPhee
Fenn Martin
Leon McAllister
Jim Mulcahey
Virginia Mulcaster
Michael Overmars
Catherine Partridge
Margaret Partridge
Gina Penny
Chantal Peppin
Grady Poe
Larry Roberts
Janet Robicheau
Mark Sears
Heather Smith

Fred Spekeen
Mike Stewart
Arwen Sweet
Tom Van Oirschot
Bill Van de Sande
Jeff Van Zwol

JoAnne Van Zwol
Jenny Van Zwol
Coady Webb
Henri Wesselink
Alana Wilson
Doven Watson

Bruce Partridge

In the early days, we would never say no to a job, even if it meant ferrying a tree to an island.

Gardening essays

Holly tackles clay and rock.

PVN tackles clay and rock

Soil is something that forms in nature beneath natural vegetation. It is a slow process by which the deep roots of the plants bring up nutrients to the leaves, which then drop off in Autumn to enrich the ground. Animals and insects burrow through the rotting leaves, stirring and loosening the soil which allows air and water to penetrate easily.

One of the least-understood facts concerning plant growth is that roots have to have plentiful air as well as water. Roots breathe oxygen and give off carbon dioxide. If they can't breathe, they die. Plants die more quickly from lack of air in the soil than they do from lack of water.

It didn't take the Pleasant Valley Nurseries landscape crew long to find out that soils in this part of the province—running heavily to clay and rocks—didn't have much air in them. Around old farm houses and country places the soil wasn't too bad and could be worked, but these were rarely the people who hired us. At that time, new houses were built by digging out a cavernous hole for the basement using a bulldozer. The horrid clay subsoil that came out of the excavation was spread all around the house, then shaped and packed down into ridges and terraces. The whole mess was probably covered with a few inches of topsoil which may or may not have been stockpiled before construction began. Then the proud owners, with visions in their heads of towering maples and heavily laden fruit trees, would call in the landscapers.

We might as well have tried to plant trees in the road. The clay was pressed solid as far down as we could get with pick and shovel, while a rototiller simply bucked and bounced off the rocks, literally striking sparks. Mixing in peat moss and manure and various fertilizers helped a little, but our early efforts at planting were less than spectacular. What to do?

This is when Henri and Dave Hoar, the landscape foreman at the time, discovered the raised planting bed. Maybe they invented it; I'm not sure. At any rate, with the raised beds our success rate improved dramatically.

The concept was simple—I should have thought of it myself. We would bust up the existing stuff (I hesitate to call it soil) with shovel, pick and rototiller, and mix in some peat moss and other amendments. Then we would bury the whole area in a layer of loose topsoil. If we made beds big enough, we could build them up a foot or more in the widest places, then mix in more amendments. Beds could be pleasantly curved and contoured. This allowed planting of plant groupings—smaller ones in front—which was much more interesting than everything all in a row.

Our plantings began to grow nicely and capture attention. Demand for our services grew.

We purchased the topsoil we used from local truckers, who delivered it. It generally came off worn-out and abandoned farm fields and varied greatly in consistency and workability—everything from light sand to fairly heavy clay. The only things these soils had in common were usually no rocks and usually no fertility.

After piling the topsoil up on planting beds we rototilled in all the peat moss, limestone, manure and fertilizer that the job could afford. The manure was generally commercially-bagged sheep or cow manure and too expensive to use in the quantity we would have liked. When we could get quantities of clean barnyard manure, we used it. We supplemented with slow-release granular fertilizer to feed the plants until the manure kicked in.

Soil was warm in raised beds and plants were well above the cold, wet and often waterlogged ground underneath. Things really began to grow.

Still, though the raised beds were great for shrubs and perennials, trees could only root down as far as the bed was deep. Since soil in the beds was quite fertile, these trees would grow nicely for many years, and achieve a respectable size, but remain shallow-rooted. Eventually all the soil in the bed was tied up tightly with tree roots. Bruce Davidson, who landscaped with us for many years, used to joke that if the wind blew strongly enough, the whole bed would tip over—which was not far from the truth.

For the sake of the trees, of which we planted hundreds every year and hoped would be our legacy, we needed to loosen up the soil more deeply than we could do it with the tools we had. This we arranged by contracting a backhoe to come in and crumble up the soil to the depth of two feet or so. We could then mix in organic matter to keep it loose, smooth it off, and pile on the topsoil. This would result in a total depth of loose soil of at least three feet—enough to make any tree happy.

At the same time as we were building and planting raised beds we began to use bark mulch. This was at first somewhat controversial because many customers feared that the mulch would attract bugs. This it did, but only good bugs that live in bark mulch and help to build soil. The mulch kept down the weeds, kept the beds from drying out, protected the soil from caking and erosion, moderated freezing and thawing and, with fertilizer, rotted slowly to enrich the soil, just like the leaves on the forest floor. Plants loved it and seemed more colourful against the dark mulch.

Once or twice we tried plantings without mulch, but the soil dried out and the only plants that grew well were the weeds. On certain sites we tried other mulches such as gravel over landscape fabric or hay or straw, but shredded tree bark was the easiest and worked the best.

We were figuring things out, and when we planted a tree it grew. Many people bought trees at our garden centre which they intended to plant themselves. Usually they didn't plan to hire a backhoe and weren't accustomed to back-breaking labour. We tried to make it easy and promoted the raised bed, or at least the raised mound technique, to anyone planting their own tree. We instructed everyone to plant their trees in spots built up higher than the ground around. The best was a sizable raised bed featuring the tree and maybe a couple of shrubs that might be taken out when the tree got too big, and some perennials. This gave the tree lots of room and good soil and people were surprised at how fast a tree could grow here. Next best was a circle three to six feet in diameter and built up above the general ground level with good soil.

We had a handout that showed how to do the planting, including how to stake a tree so it didn't blow over. Customers were relieved that they wouldn't have to excavate a deep hole or remove any ground—just take off the sod and loosen the ground underneath, then pile on the topsoil.

These instructions were not only to help people with their trees, but also for our own protection. We guaranteed our trees, and we were quite sure that nearly every tree we replaced had been planted too deeply and watered so frequently and heavily that its roots suffocated. A raised bed or planting circle made it difficult to overwater and, as gardeners caught on, we replaced fewer trees.

Fertilizers

You can nearly always assume that soils in this part of Nova Scotia are acidic and low in fertility and need some help. Most soil is worn out ex-farmland. Even soil covered with forest was usually cleared fields and pastures a couple of generations back. Acid rain, which appears to be with us to stay, has dissolved and washed out any nutrients that remained and left the soil strongly acidic.

Garden centres and farm stores sell a wide variety of products to make soil fertile again. The most immediate concern is to neutralize the acidity of, or "sweeten", the soil. In acidic soil important nutrients are tied up and unavailable to plants. Though wood ashes or compost or sea shells or certain other materials will reduce soil acidity, we found it convenient to use powdered limestone, which is cheap and sold everywhere. Simply throw or spread it over the surface of the soil as evenly as possible, and mix it in before planting. It can also be spread over lawns, which appreciate it, or around established plants. It doesn't burn. Since it is a natural product and the supply appears to be inexhaustible, we could consider it "organic". Not so, fertilizer.

Well, there certainly are organic fertilizers, and more every year, but I am thinking of the old granular, or "farm" fertilizers. These were fifty-pound bags comprised of three nutrients—nitrogen, phosphorus, and potassium—in ratios such as 6-12-12 or 17-17-17. Farm fertilizers supplied plenty of the three nutrients most needed by plants and most likely to be lacking in the soil, and were cheap and powerful. Compared to animal manure, they were like whisky compared to beer. A little went a long way.

In the early days of Pleasant Valley Nurseries, governments and garden centres promoted granular chemical fertilizers. There was no stigma to using them. The invention of these fertilizers was, in fact, a big part of the worldwide "green revolution", and they could give amazing results. Everyone wanted them. It was difficult to promote organic.

Time, of course, showed the problems of using chemical fertilizers year after year. The soil requires a certain level of organic matter to keep it loose and to provide nutrients that are not found in a bag of fertilizer. Continual use of chemical fertilizer eventually burns up all the organic matter in the soil, which leads to infertility and erosion. It became obvious that these fertilizers should only be used in combination with adequate amounts of organic materials. If this is the case, they are still useful as a convenient way to boost soil fertility quickly.

In recent times, the pendulum has swung the other way. Gardeners and people in general have become better informed and insist that soils and crops be organic. Chemical fertilizer, though it really contains no dangerous substances, is equated with chemical pesticides and is nearly as dead as the dodo. Garden centres sell myriads of organic plant supplements, fertilizers, and plant amendments, and it's risky to suggest chemicals.

By and large this is a good thing, as long as people can afford organics and use enough. Trendy organics are expensive and gardening has become a pricey proposition except for those who can get hold of old-fashioned barnyard manure or lots of compost. No question that organic fertilizers are long-lasting and good for the soil. They are especially good in the vegetable garden or other areas where food is grown.

While organic fertilizers and soil amendments are just as desirable in ornamental plantings, they can be more trouble to use than chemical fertilizers, and require more work and dedication—not to mention money. Manures and composts are bulky and heavy. Also, you have to rake the bark mulch off the beds before spreading the fertilizer, and then put it back. For homeowners or businesses that want to keep the work of fertilizing to a minimum, the combination of bark and chemical fertilizer is effective and ecologically sound.

In this case, simply throw a good, slow-release granular fertilizer into the bark mulch around the plants once a year. Jiggle the bark a little with a rake so the granules settle in a bit. Rain washes the fertilizer through the bark to where the plants can use it. The fertilizer supplies nutrients while decomposing bark supplies organic matter. Soil in planting beds managed this way stays healthy and workable. Fertilizer does cause bark mulch to rot away more quickly, though, so you must top it up when it gets thin.

To summarize, use raised beds, mulch, organic matter and limestone, and maybe a few handfuls of chemical fertilizer in your ornamental beds; maybe skip the chemical fertilizer where you are growing things to eat. With very few exceptions, this will suit anything you are likely to plant.

Happy gardening.

Planting a tree

People plant trees everywhere in Nova Scotia, but in the Northeast of the province, special procedures apply. If you find a tag with planting instructions on the tree you just bought, throw it out. It was undoubtedly written in California for planting in a hot, dry climate. The combination of damp climate and tight clay soil found here requires a different approach.

To begin with, don't think that you must plant the tree in a bowl-shaped depression that catches water, or dig the roots deep into the ground. Either way, the soil will be too wet and heavy around the roots, and they will suffocate. To become established quickly and grow well, trees need to be planted shallowly in raised beds or mounds. When the tree is positioned properly, the roots will grow down to where they want to be. If you place the roots too deep in the ground, they can't grow back up. We had a tree at the garden centre that literally just stood on the parking lot for a planting demonstration, with the roots lightly covered with soil. It grew.

The tree planting spot is a variation of the raised bed that we advocate for anything you plant.

If you take a look at trees in the woods, you will see that the tree flares out and the roots begin at ground level. Furthermore, in wet areas, trees are invariably growing on raised humps or hillocks. When planting a tree, you should copy these conditions.

Prepare a raised bed or circle by skimming off the sod, breaking up the soil underneath and piling on extra topsoil. Then turn the whole works, mix in peat moss and compost or manure, and rake it up to form a planting mound. You might mix in a shovelful of limestone and a cup of garden fertilizer as well to get the tree off to a quick start. This mound could be a raised bed big enough for the tree and a few shrubs or perennials, or simply a circle at least three feet wide—preferably four or five or bigger if you are ambitious. Tree roots in our soils grow wide rather than deep. Build up the planting spot as high as possible without it looking silly.

Now, planting is easy. With the soil in the mound deep and loose, you only have to dig out enough from the top of the mound to set the tree in. You can almost do it with your bare hands. If the tree is in a pot, that is the size of the hole you dig from the centre of the mound. If the tree is bare root, you dig out enough to accommodate the roots when the tree is set so that it flares out as it enters the ground.

Put the soil you take out into a bucket or wheelbarrow. Remove the potted tree from its pot and rough up the roots with a spade or trowel—an inch or so around the root ball should do it. If the tree is bare root, trim any broken or damaged roots.

Now, position the tree like the one in the woods, with the roots just beginning to flare out at ground level, or with the top surface of the root ball just underneath the top of the mound. Fill back in around the roots with the soil you took out.

Just before the soil is all back in, water the tree with a bucket—carefully, so as not to wash the soil around. Finish putting the soil back in.

You now will notice that, if you don't stay holding the tree, the wind is going to blow it down sooner or later. Correct. You must stake the tree by driving a pointed 2 by 2 or a thin fence post solidly down through the roots close alongside the trunk of the tree. Have someone tilt the tree aside so you don't hit it with the pounder. The stake should be long enough that it ends up just below the first branches.

Then attach the tree to the stake with a strong, flexible plastic strap or a piece of old garden hose wrapped in a figure 8 around the tree and screwed or nailed to the stake. Use another stake on the other side of the tree if the tree is large.

Rake the circle nicely and put on four or five inches of bark mulch to conserve moisture and discourage grass and weeds. Done.

Let the tree grow one summer. In case of prolonged drought, water deeply maybe once a week. Anytime you can poke your finger through the mulch and feel dampness, the tree is OK. Eager gardeners can easily overwater a newly planted tree in our climate and soil, thinking it will grow faster. Some water every day believing that water is some kind of fertilizer. This quickly drives air out of the soil and the roots suffocate. To make things worse, this tree wilts exactly like one that is too dry. A tree that has wilted from dryness will perk up within hours of being watered. One that has wilted from over-watering is finished.

We humans tend to understand animals better than trees. No one would keep pouring water down the throat of a puppy in case it was thirsty. Enough wrist slapping.

Okay: your tree wasn't over watered and looks good in the Spring. Push it back and forth a little bit. If it seems well connected to the ground, you can remove the stake.

In the landscape, trees are a special case. Shrubs and flowers can grow and flourish in very little soil, but not trees. In the forest the good soil goes on and on and trees can spread their roots as far as they want. Soil in the yards around our homes is all too often a different matter. Sometimes, you can hardly call it soil. Maybe it was soil once, but that was before it was covered with subsoil from the basement excavation and packed down by heavy equipment.

If this is the case, and you want to plant a tree that will live a hundred years, you must lay out a generous-sized bed and have a backhoe or small excavator turn the sod upside down and break up the hardpan beneath the bed to a depth of about two feet. Ideally, you can get the operator to stir in as much manure and peat moss as you can get your hands on to keep the soil loose. After that, pile on the topsoil and make the raised bed. The bed can be large enough to contain the tree and an arrangement of shrubs and flowers. The tree by now will be on top of two to three feet of loose soil and will grow big and healthy, and live a long time. Your grandchildren will thank you.

Henri worked out a planting strategy that works very well for large numbers of small trees, as in windbreaks. We call it the hay bale technique. At each spot where you want to plant a tree, lay two hay bales on the ground up tight to one another. This doesn't

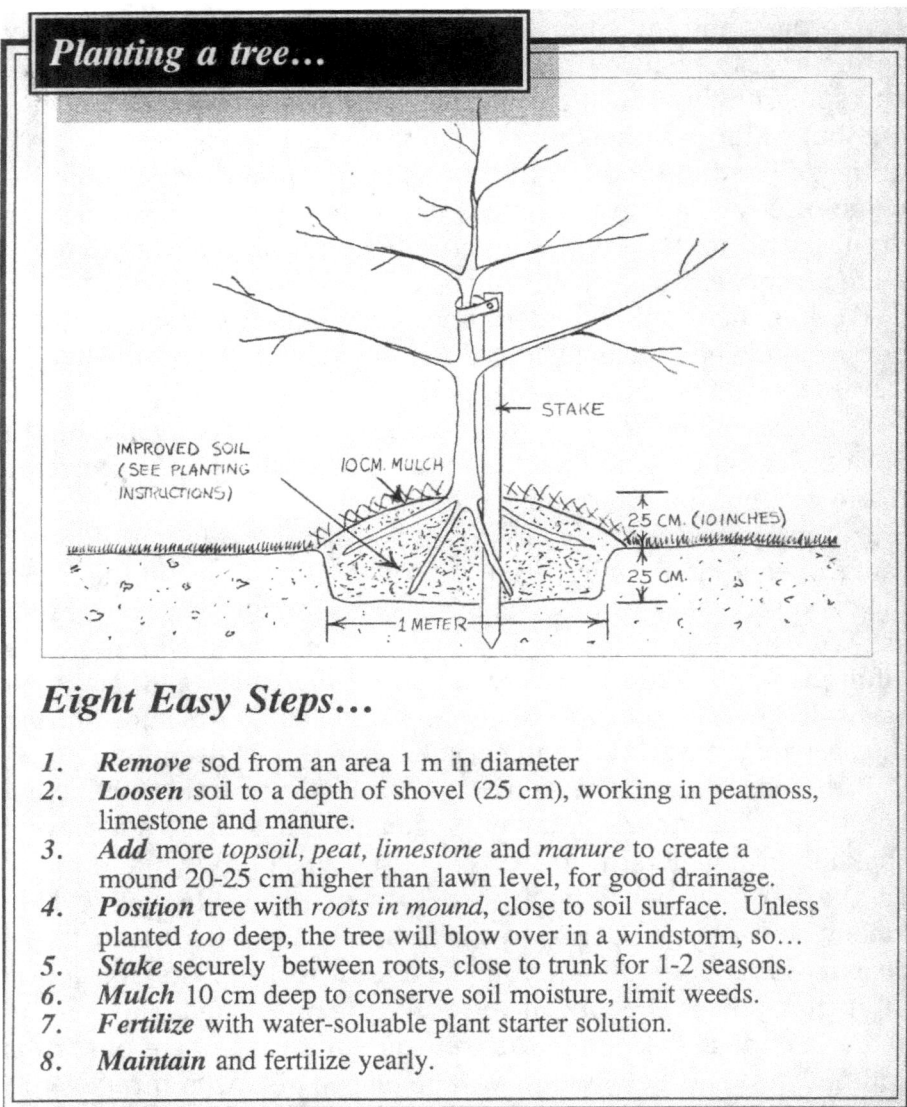

Eight Easy Steps...

1. **Remove** sod from an area 1 m in diameter
2. **Loosen** soil to a depth of shovel (25 cm), working in peatmoss, limestone and manure.
3. **Add** more *topsoil, peat, limestone* and *manure* to create a mound 20-25 cm higher than lawn level, for good drainage.
4. **Position** tree with *roots in mound*, close to soil surface. Unless planted *too* deep, the tree will blow over in a windstorm, so...
5. **Stake** securely between roots, close to trunk for 1-2 seasons.
6. **Mulch** 10 cm deep to conserve soil moisture, limit weeds.
7. **Fertilize** with water-soluable plant starter solution.
8. **Maintain** and fertilize yearly.

have to be high quality hay. You can often find cheap bales that are old or have been spoiled by rain. Leave the bales in place for an entire season to smother the grass or weeds underneath.

Borderline Hardy in 5b

The following spring, roll the bales aside. At this point, the ground underneath is bare and has been enriched by decomposing hay. It is probably full of earthworms—a good sign.

Plant the little tree in this spot. Break up leftover hay bales and arrange them around the newly-planted tree to keep away encroaching grass and weeds. Young trees pampered like this get off to a strong start and develop quickly.

A strong start is important for anything you plant.

Bruce Partridge

Shade trees

Henri and I took great interest in growing and selling shade and ornamental trees. At the nursery, Henri grew a wide variety. We were also intrigued by exotic and unusual tree species that other nurseries offered. We ordered many of these and received them with our Spring shipment of plants from Ontario. We were eager to plant them and see how they would do in Antigonish.

Some of these trees did well, but others were disappointing. Trees from other countries, other climates and other growing zones had a way of dying abruptly in a bad winter a few years down the road. Oddly enough, it didn't seem to be the coldest winters that killed them. It was the winters when the temperature bounced up and down from well above 0°C to well below. This isn't unusual in Nova Scotia.

The worst combination was a thaw and mild weather lasting two or three weeks in the middle of winter, followed by a sharp freeze. Trees that could easily tolerate the coldest temperatures we get here, if it *stayed* cold, couldn't take the fluctuation. It seems that the mild spell would get the sap flowing, then the cold snap would kill them. Some imported trees could survive our winters, but just didn't grow very well. Some others, though, did fine.

The most remarkable of imported trees was the Norway maple. It grew just like it was born here. On top of that, it was exceptionally variable and, besides green, could be had in red and yellow or a combination. Gardeners know the red-leafed one as the Crimson King. The golden one—Princeton Gold—also became very popular. You could spot them in people's yards a mile away.

Then there was the Harlequin, which had a green leaf edged in white. There were several green selections and a couple that were green but red at the tips. In the early years at PVN I think we sold more Norway maple cultivars than any other tree.

The only other imported trees I can think of that we sold regularly were the horse chestnut and the English Oak—both of which Henri grew in Lakevale from seed—and the European beech.

Little by little, we learned that there were no better trees to plant than the ones that grew here naturally. The imports were starting to have problems—even the Norway maples. These trees, which never had outstanding Fall colour in the first place, now suffered from tar spot—black blotches on the leaves that were ugly and caused them to drop early. They were also weak-wooded and easily broken in storms. Finally, it became clear that Norway maples could be weedy and aggressive. They produced large quantities of seed that came up in hedges and cracks in the sidewalk, and large crops of seedlings that were crowding out native maples in the woods.

As for the horse chestnut, it was afflicted with a fungus which didn't impair the growth much, but caused the leaves to turn brown and unsightly by August. We continued to grow and sell them, though, because they were more tolerant of salt spray than any other tree and could be planted next to the seashore. The European beech and English oak were and are still dependable and good-looking, but uncommonly slow-growing.

We were shifting our attention to native species in the Lakevale nursery. Other nurseries—even the big ones in Ontario—were focusing more and more on the natives.

Our native trees—the maples, ash, oak, and birch, to list the most familiar—are as nice as any trees in the world. Maybe we don't get excited because they are everywhere, and they are green —not red or yellow or striped. It is they, though, that set the woods ablaze with colour in the Fall. At that time of year, the beauty of our forests is one of the wonders of the world.

Best of all, natives grow here as if they were, well, native. They can reach an impressive size under the right conditions, may live to be several hundred years old, and don't up and die in a bad winter. In Europe, our native trees are their exotics. Our maples are highly sought after and, in an ironic turn of the tables, the native red oak has become an invasive pest in parts of Europe.

Bruce Partridge

Shade trees in the nursery

Here in Nova Scotia, what I am saying is that our most reliable trees are those that grow here naturally. I guess that should come as no surprise, but it seems to be human nature to want something different. My advice to anyone planting trees is to plant the trusty natives first—red and sugar maple, red oak, paper or yellow birch, ironwood, and probably white ash, though there is an insect heading this way that is killing the ash as it goes.

At one time, the American elm shaded farms, river valleys and streets of towns and villages, including Antigonish, and would have been a good choice for a large property. Henri has lately been testing and evaluating new, disease-resistant clones of the American elm and one day soon the elm may be a good choice again. Meanwhile, we all know what the bark beetle and the elm disease did to the elms, and hope this will not be the fate of the ash.

By the way, the native red maple is a green tree (*Acer rubrum*), which turns brilliant red or orange in our woods in the Fall. It is not the Crimson King, which has dark red leaves all summer and is an imported variety of Norway maple, (*Acer platanoides*). The leaves of the Crimson King turn black in Fall and look—as Henri says—like bat wings.

Plant sugar maple, yellow birch, and ironwood where the soil is reasonably deep and fertile. None of the three tolerates dry soil—especially the ironwood. All require good drainage. In dry locations, try the red oak or the white birch. In poorly-drained ground, the best bets are the white or green ash, the red maple or the white birch, started in elevated mounds. Don't even consider the weeping willow. It belongs beside farm ponds or in fertile river bottoms.

Finally, please don't plant an introduced tree or, even worse, a fruit tree, to commemorate the birth of a child or some other weighty event. These trees have a perverse habit of dying prematurely or simply losing branches and looking terrible from all that responsibility. Play it safe with a native. An apple tree might be okay if it is not a dwarf.

Once you have the basic trees in place, then it is time to try some colourful imports if you wish. There are many smaller flowering and ornamental trees, some native and some imported, which are good in the landscape. My personal favourites are the flowering crabapples, of which there are hundreds of selections, but there are also the Japanese maples, tree lilacs, mountain ashes, hawthorns, flowering dogwoods, magnolias and others to choose from.

If you like trees, this is where things get interesting (and expensive). What better way to spend your money, though?

The author, as a young man, with an apple tree from the nursery.

Fruit trees

At Pleasant Valley Nurseries we offered a good selection of fruit trees with varieties we deemed the most suitable for our area. Henri's very first foray into horticulture in Nova Scotia was grafting and growing apple trees. We always had some of our own trees to sell, and also sold trees produced by larger nurseries.

We had a formidable mentor living in Bayfield near Antigonish. Roy Hulbert came from an apple-growing family in Massachusetts that had supplied the Boston market with apples for generations. Roy lived and breathed apples and kept an impeccable orchard of several hundred trees at home. He was a walking encyclopedia on the subject, including the pros and cons of every variety grown in North America since 1900. With Roy's help, advice from the experts in Kentville, and no small amount of reading and study, we kept up on the latest varieties as well as the old-fashioned ones, and their cultural requirements. Growing fruit is not a simple thing, and we were very determined that customers would be successful with our trees.

Not everyone knows that nearly all fruit trees are grafted. Very few are raised from seed. This is because no two trees raised from seed are ever exactly alike. If you plant seeds taken from a nice apple—let's say a McIntosh—and grow them into trees, each one will be different and not one will be a McIntosh. This is because a seedling is a result of a cross between two parents, and combines characteristics from each, just like the children of human parents. No two are ever alike or exactly like either of their parents. Seedling trees are seldom as good as their parents. I won't extend that observation to children.

When grafting, you can use fruit trees raised from seed as the lower part, or rootstock, of the tree. The seedling is grown to the appropriate size, then cut off close to the ground and a piece of another tree—the scion—spliced or "grafted" onto it. The scion is a bud or a twig taken from the variety of tree that you wish to grow. The graft heals and the scion grows to become the entire top of the tree, genetically identical to and producing the same fruit as the tree it came from. The rootstock provides the roots and the scion provides the top of the tree and the fruit. If the scion came from a McIntosh tree, the new tree will produce McIntosh apples. It is interesting that the original McIntosh apple was a wild tree discovered in Ontario in 1811. Every McIntosh tree grown since then comes from a piece of a McIntosh tree cut from a piece of a McIntosh tree cut from a piece of a McIntosh tree, all the way back to that tree discovered in 1811.

Another sometimes confusing concept is that apple trees, and some other fruit trees, can be grafted onto size-controlling rootstocks. If an apple is grafted onto an apple seedling it will eventually grow into a full-size, or "standard" size tree. With age, this can be huge, making pruning and picking quite difficult. Commercial growers want a smaller tree that is easier to manage. Almost all apple trees sold these days are grafted onto size-controlling rootstocks. These are apple selections that when used as a rootstock for grafting, inhibit the growth of the tree and its ultimate size. Many size-controlling rootstocks have been developed by commercial nurseries and agricultural research facilities all over the world.

Picking the appropriate rootstock, you can produce an apple tree that is almost as big as a standard, or one that is so small you can pick the apples while standing on the ground. The intermediate sizes are called semi-standard, or semi-dwarf and the small ones are dwarf. The dwarf trees obviously are suited to commercial culture because they are easily tended and picked, and can be planted close together, like a hedge. They would also seem to be suited to small gardens and properties in towns, but it isn't quite that simple.

Dwarf trees, to succeed, need more care and better soil than the larger-growing trees. The dwarfing rootstock is slow to root strongly, and a well-developed tree with a full crop of apples might tip right over in the wind. Consequently, dwarf trees need to be solidly staked, sometimes for their entire life. In addition, they do not compete well with tough grass and weeds and must be mulched underneath or kept cleanly cultivated.

Commercial orchards are established on deep, fertile soil so dwarf trees root well. How many of us, however, live in places with deep, fertile soil? If we have an area at home where the soil is good and fertile, however, such as a vegetable garden, or a prepared planting bed, a dwarf tree might be just the thing. It might be planted along the northern edge of the garden, so as not to shade the vegetables, and do quite well if it were staked and mulched.

Gardeners coming to PVN in the early days to buy apple trees often asked for dwarf trees. These were inevitably planted in circles in the grass, and we began to notice that they didn't do very well, and that our customers weren't happy. The poor performance was, of course, due to poor soil—most often bulldozed clay—and marginal growing conditions where they were planted. After listening to so many sad stories and complaints from people who had planted dwarfs, I was frightened to recommend anything but semi-dwarfs, which are tougher trees all around. People buying semi-dwarfs might complain someday that the tree got too big, but that's better than one that didn't grow at all.

Pollination is an issue with all fruit trees, and apples are no exception. In most cases, it is necessary to have two apple trees of *different* varieties to insure cross-pollination and fruit production. Customers probably thought that this was a ruse to sell them two trees instead of one, but it is simply a biological fact. Bees do the work, of course, but the pollen from one variety of apple won't pollinate the flowers of the same variety, so—no fruit.

No fruit is unusual with apples, however, because a wild tree nearby or one in a neighbour's yard, or even an ornamental crabapple can provide the pollen. Customers usually bought two trees anyway. A few apple varieties are no good as pollinators. If you want a Gravenstein, you'll need three trees.

Pollination requirements of apple trees are quite straightforward, but pollination of other fruit trees can get messy. Pears are okay. As with apples, you just need two trees of different varieties that bloom at the same time. Sweet cherries are the same, though some varieties are self-pollinating and can bear fruit all alone. Sour or pie cherries and peaches are self-pollinating—you only need one tree.

Plum pollination is a nightmare. First of all, there are two species of plums commonly sold, the European and the Japanese. The European plums are usually oblong and purple or blue. The Japanese plums are round and red or yellow. Pollination-wise, the European and Japanese plums are not compatible. There are also hybrid plums, which are Japanese plums usually crossed with wild North American plums. Some of these will cross with some Japanese plums; some won't. Japanese plums will cross with some other Japanese plums, but not all of them. Any European plum will cross with any other European, and some of them are self-pollinating.

Nurseries growing plums print pollination charts to show which plum varieties are compatible. At PVN we had three of these charts from different sources, each contradicting the others. I encouraged people to buy a few varieties, just to be sure.

Different types of fruit trees require different types of management, but their soil requirements are approximately the same. Suitable soil conditions are of critical importance in a fruit tree planting. The newly planted tree must take off quickly and continue to grow steadily at a good rate. Any tree whose growth is inhibited by poor soil is sure to be attacked by every disease and insect going and will be very unlikely to thrive.

People who have decided to plant fruit trees are generally impatient to get them in the ground and growing. Prepare your ground well before you begin. It may be hard to wait, but a summer spent preparing the ground will put you years ahead in the long run. If you dig in limestone and manure, it will have time to break down and become effective. Repeated tilling or, better yet, growing cover crops like buckwheat and tilling, or mulching the area with grass clippings or old hay, will enrich the soil and make sure that problem grasses or weeds are all dead. Then put in the trees.

All fruit trees need a well-drained soil. This is number one. No fruit tree will be happy in wet soil. Some soils are naturally well-drained. Others can be made so by mounding or drains.

The fact that the land is sloping has no bearing on whether or not the soil is well-drained. 'Well-drained' means that water from rain or melting snow passes through the soil to deeper layers at an adequate rate. Tree roots in the soil require oxygen as well as, or maybe more than, water. Water that is descending through the soil carries oxygen with it. A tree in this soil can continue to grow and thrive even if it rains for a month. Water trapped in poorly-drained soil does not move. It quickly loses its oxygen. Tree roots suffocate and the tree struggles or dies.

The wettest time in these parts is the very early Spring, when it is raining and the snow is melting. There are no leaves on the trees yet and we are scarcely aware that they are alive. They are, though, and if all that water doesn't continue to pass down through the soil, those roots will die. It only takes a couple of days. The same soil may dry out in warmer weather, allowing trees to grow fine for a while. It was common to hear stories at the garden centre of trees that had been planted in the Spring, done well through the summer, then turned up dead the following Spring. The culprit was almost always poor drainage, unless rabbits or mice had girdled them.

You can mitigate poor soil drainage by heaping the soil up in the area to be planted. You can see that orchards on old farms were planted in long, elevated mounds eight feet wide or more. Today, you could do that easily with an excavator.

Less ambitious plantings, of course can be in elevated areas formed up by hand or with smaller machinery. Even in well-drained soil it is a good idea to build it up some. The soil stays warmer that way—plantings should be in full sun—and the tree grows faster. It will root deeper if it wants to.

The second requirement for good growth of fruit trees is good soil fertility. Most soils in Nova Scotia—even most former agricultural soils—are worn out as far as nutrients are concerned. Nutrients are depleted by cropping and leached out by acid rain, or tied up in acid ground and unavailable to plants. Once you have good soil drainage, it's time to work on fertility.

Soil to which nothing has been added is almost sure to be too acidic for good growth of fruit trees. In an acid soil, important nutrients such as phosphorus are unavailable to plants. All fruit trees enjoy a soil that is neutral—neither strongly acidic nor strongly alkaline. Neutralize acid ground by applying a soil sweetener, usually ground limestone. Ground limestone is dusty but quite benign. It isn't poisonous and won't burn vegetation. You can spread it at any time of year, but it requires at least a year to take full effect. The more you work it into the soil, the better. An application of limestone is good for a few years, so you don't have to repeat it annually. A soil test will determine how much to use, though it is hard to overdo it. Besides sweetening the soil, limestone supplies quantities of calcium and sometimes magnesium—important plant nutrients. In some situations, you can use materials such as wood ash, seashells or compost to sweeten the soil.

The nutrients trees use in by far the largest quantities are the big three—nitrogen, phosphorus, and potassium. In newly-broken ground, these are almost certain to be deficient. Commercial granular fertilizers are made up of these three nutrients in varying ratios. You may apply these to quickly bring the soil fertility to where it should be. If the soil has enough organic matter in it, and has been limed, the levels of all other essential plant nutrients are probably okay for now. The best way to find out how much fertilizer to apply is a soil test. The Departments of Agriculture can explain tests, and what their results mean.

Organic fertilizers and manures are always good. Any type of barnyard manure, compost, grass clippings, seaweed, shells, decomposed hay or straw are worth their weight in gold. Use all you can get. You can use sawdust, wood shavings, and bark, but only if you supplement them with extra nitrogen from granular fertilizer or manure. You can bring any soil up to snuff and maintain it with organic fertilizers; it just takes a while before the organic matter begins to break down and release nutrients.

Borderline Hardy in 5b

If soil is well-drained, sweet, and high in nutrients, any fruit tree —any plant at all, for that matter—is going to grow.

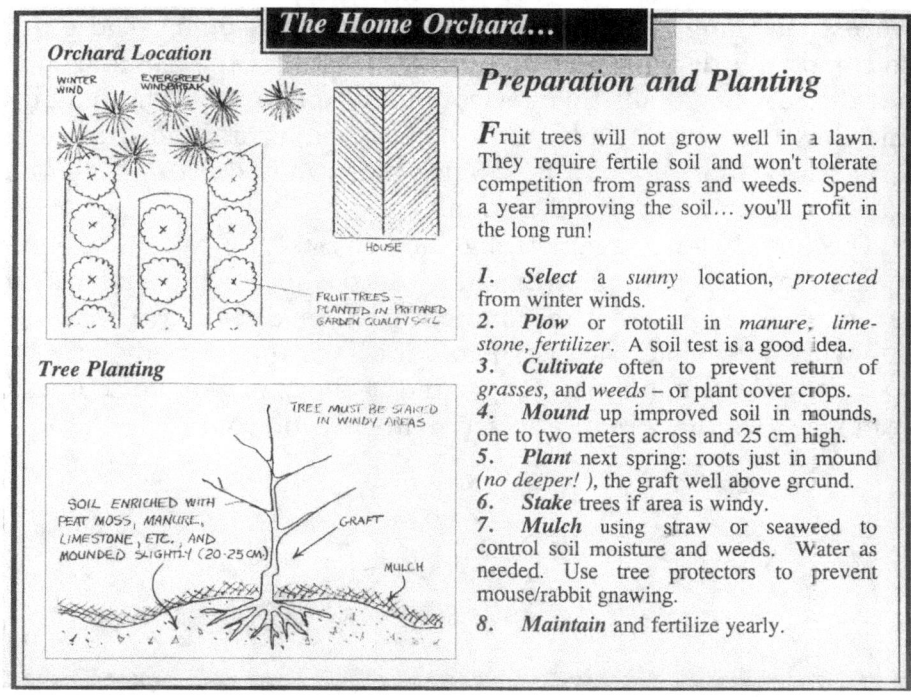

The Home Orchard...

Orchard Location

Tree Planting

Preparation and Planting

Fruit trees will not grow well in a lawn. They require fertile soil and won't tolerate competition from grass and weeds. Spend a year improving the soil... you'll profit in the long run!

1. *Select* a *sunny* location, *protected* from winter winds.
2. *Plow* or rototill in *manure, limestone, fertilizer*. A soil test is a good idea.
3. *Cultivate* often to prevent return of *grasses*, and *weeds* – or plant cover crops.
4. *Mound* up improved soil in mounds, one to two meters across and 25 cm high.
5. *Plant* next spring: roots just in mound (*no deeper!*), the graft well above ground.
6. *Stake* trees if area is windy.
7. *Mulch* using straw or seaweed to control soil moisture and weeds. Water as needed. Use tree protectors to prevent mouse/rabbit gnawing.
8. *Maintain* and fertilize yearly.

One last observation concerning fruit trees and nutrition: apples, pears, and European plums grow well in rich soil. Cherries and peaches, and sometimes the Japanese plums, grow *too* well in rich soil and don't want to slow down to get ready for winter. If you are planting these, the soil should be well-drained but not too fertile. Use organic fertilizers like manure or compost and just enough to keep the soil crumbly and loose. Mulch fruit trees when they are young with hay or straw to smother out grass and weeds.

Too many insects and diseases to mention attack fruit trees, but most of them don't do much harm. If the tree is growing vigorously, it can tolerate quite a bit of damage to the leaves, and keep growing new ones. I believe that, in most cases, all you need in the way of insecticides is Bt (*bacillus thuringiensis*) for caterpillars and insecticidal soap for aphids. Both are quite safe to use.

Bruce Partridge

There is a little green worm—the looper or leaf roller—that chews the leaves up badly when they are first coming out. Bt takes care of him. It also works against tent caterpillars. If you see the leaves becoming all crinkled up, it is probably aphids. These are soft-bodied little bugs that live in colonies under the leaf and suck out the sap. Soap kills them. If you notice lots of ants climbing up and down the tree trunk, put a band of paper around the trunk with sticky Tanglefoot on it to block them. Ants don't damage the tree, but they spread aphids around.

The best defence against bugs and diseases is to take a good look at your trees frequently, and if you see anything peculiar, find out what it is and what to do about it. After one or two seasons, you will know what to expect before it comes and be ready for it.

If you have a good piece of ground in the sun, why not put in a fruit tree? There is great satisfaction in growing your own.

Nut trees

I believe I see the popularity circle of nut trees coming around again. Maybe it has never stopped. Nut trees were almost where I started when I bought my first place, a 90-year-old schoolhouse with half an acre of land in Black Avon, Antigonish County. Now I see my young neighbour, Sandy Forbes, and his friends eagerly planting nut trees just as I did. They are much more scientific and methodical than I was, though, and studied up on nut tree culture before they started. Of course, they have us old PVN geezers, who already made all the mistakes, to advise them.

Surprisingly, Sandy and his friends get most of their trees from the same nursery that I did—the E. Grimo Nut Nursery near St. Catherines, Ontario. There were other nut nurseries, mostly also centred around St. Catherines, but E. Grimo was *el Primo*.

This is really going to hurt to reveal how naive and clueless I was when I started planting nut trees. My idea was to purchase trees and plant them among the spruces, birch, ash and maple growing in the woods behind my place. I thought that there must be good soil in the woods. After all, there were already trees growing there that looked pretty good.

There were at least three things wrong with my plan. First was that it was going to be a couple of years yet before I learned how sour and worn out the soil could be in the woods—which was generally used-up farm fields grown up in trees.

The second thing wrong with my plan was that I disregarded the competition underground from the roots of existing trees, and the competition above-ground from the tree canopy which blocked too much sunlight

The third mistake was that I ignored the curious wild animals that never fail to chew on a newly-planted tree just to see if they like it. Deer, rabbits, porcupines and mice all had a taste, and this didn't do the trees any good at all.

Well, as they say, hindsight is 20-20, and I might have known that those trees—mostly black walnut—wouldn't do well where I planted them. To their credit, though, they took quite a few years to die. They leafed out bravely each Spring, but never grew an inch. My 20-20 hindsight also tells me, though, that I had the answer but didn't know it.

The trees I ordered from Ontario shipped in the Spring. I think the Grimo nursery delayed shipping trees to the Maritimes because they realized that Spring was slow here. Trees must have arrived in May, because I remember that the soil in the garden was thawed when they came.

It was exciting to open the box. At that time of year, though, I had only a vague idea of where to plant them all, and little time to get the planting spots ready, so I "heeled" them into the warm rich soil of the vegetable garden. That will keep them until Fall, I figured, and then I will put them their permanent spots.

I realize now that those trees never intended to leave the garden. They shot up amazing shoots of growth, sometimes two or three feet in just a couple of months. If I had left them there, they might have been large trees in only a few years. In order to play God, though, and put them where I wanted them, I dug them mercilessly out of the garden and transplanted them into the woods where, as I mentioned earlier, they never grew again.

Later on, I finally did it right. I ordered a couple of young shagbark hickory trees, again from Ontario. As I had been doing, I fixed up a fertile planting spot in an old cutover and even put a circle of rocks around it. The trees, when they arrived, were very curious looking. They were only about a foot tall and each one had a tap root, like a parsnip, longer than that. I went ahead and planted them in my spot and, to my delight, they leafed out nicely and nearly doubled in size that first summer.

Winter was a different story. Rabbits found them and nibbled them back down to where they had started. Each year after that was the same. The little trees grew up pretty well during the summer, then in winter the rabbits ate them down again. This went on for three or four years, and finally I took mercy.

I dug the trees up, which proved to be a surprisingly hard job. The tree tops hadn't grown any, but the root had gone down quite a ways. I was only able to get about half of the tap root. There were no visible feeder roots and I was sure I had killed the trees.

Nevertheless, I planted them in the rich soil at the edge of the vegetable garden to recover, where to my surprise they leafed out. For a couple of years I more or less ignored them. They leafed out and that was about it. Then, one summer, they shot up several feet tall with big, handsome, glossy leaves. If they were that happy there, I wasn't going to move them again.

They are there today—fifteen or twenty feet high and growing beautifully. Later I planted three pecans and a ginkgo in the garden and they all grew big. I had to move the garden.

The conclusion is obvious. Nut trees want sun and fertile soil. It took me a few years and some dead trees to understand this, but it is obvious to you. I'll come back to this subject later.

Hardy nut trees come in all guises, from the walnuts, pecans, almonds, and hazels that we see at Christmas to hickories, beeches, butternuts, ginkgoes, pine nuts, and the not-quite-hardy chestnut. The Brazil nut is understandably not included. In Nova Scotia, you can cultivate most of these trees under the right conditions, but many are—as in the title of this book—borderline hardy.

The most commonly-grown nut trees in Nova Scotia are probably the walnuts and their allies, and the hazels. The walnuts, butternuts, heartnuts and related hybrids belong in the genus *Juglans*. Hickories and pecans are less commonly grown and belong in the genus *Carya*. Both *Juglans* and *Carya* are in the family *Juglandaceae*, whose members are known not only for their tasty hard-shelled nuts, but for a substance called juglone that they excrete from their roots into the soil to poison any competing vegetation. Juglone can be hard on vegetable or flower gardens, apple trees and some other things, so be aware when you are planting your trees. Hazel nuts are completely unrelated and don't excrete juglone.

★ NUT TREES

F900 BLACK WALNUT [*Juglans nigra*] This, native to North America, nut producer grows into a large tree. It has ornamental and timber value besides its yield of delicious nuts. Needs deep, well-drained soil to accommodate its large tap root system.

F901 CARPATHIAN WALNUT [*Juglans regia 'Carpathian'*] A hardy Persian walnut that does very well in Nova Scotia. The tree needs a deep soil to grow. The nuts are easy to open of superb eating quality. It will reach a height of 25m. (50') with a crown spread of 12m. (40').

NUT TREE PRICES:
$12.90 each $12.40 each for 3 and up

F904 HALL'S HARDY ALMOND: Delicious almond grows rapidly and bears at early age. Must be planted in sheltered location on good light soil. Nuts mature in September. For best results, plant two or more trees.   125cm — $9.90 each   3 trees and up — $9.40 each

Plant nut trees in pairs for good pollination, and in the open where they have plenty of room to spread, and so you don't have to worry about juglone. There are numerous species of walnuts and hickories and both natural and man-made hybrids of most of them. The wind pollinates them, and they require a second tree of the same species nearby for pollination. Hazels are much smaller bushy trees, but are also wind-pollinated and need a mate.

As with fruit trees, many superior nut trees have been isolated and are propagated by grafting. They all have names. Don't make the mistake of planting two grafted trees with the same name together for pollination. They are genetically the same tree and won't cross.

Walnuts and hickories are surprisingly fast growing in good soil. Once they get going they can grow four or five feet a year even in our climate. They also get rather huge, so give them plenty of room. Forty or fifty feet apart wouldn't be too much. If you are planting more than two trees it is good to group them so the air is full of pollen when the wind blows in Spring.

Put them in the best soil you have, where they will have room to grow. If you don't have an expendable vegetable garden as I did, prepare a good-sized circle for each tree. A good size is five or six feet across. Remove the sod, fertilize and work the soil as if you were going to plant vegetables. Don't forget limestone. Nut trees all want a sweet soil (neutral pH).

Nut trees, as a rule, are big and handsome and can be a good shade tree on a large property. They get as large as our big maples and ash. I know of some black walnut and butternut that are doing well in suburban yards in Antigonish. You can plant just one if you don't have room for two, but you won't get any nuts unless your neighbour has a tree. If I only had room for one or two shade trees on my property, though, I would go with the maple or oak. I'm a little wary of the borderline hardiness of many of the nut trees.

Hazels are not really a tree, but a large bushy shrub up to ten or twelve feet high. They are easily grown in Nova Scotia and can produce large crops of tasty nuts except for a couple of problems: blight and blue jays. The blight is a fungus infection that probably comes from native hazels. It makes black patches on twigs and stems and can cause big sections of the bush to dry up and die. I had a long hedge of hazels along the road in front of my house that I started from the bumper crop of nuts I got from my first two trees before the blight and the blue jays found them. The hedge eventually became quite unsightly with lots of dead wood in it. Every couple of years I cut it all down to near the ground and it all grew back healthy for a while. It still produced lots of nuts but I never got any because of the blue jays.

Once the blue jays found my hazels, they came back every summer just before the nuts were ripe. They cut off the green nuts and pecked the unripe meat out of them and didn't leave any of them to ripen. I tried every trick I could think of to stop them. One year I cut squares out of mesh onion bags and covered every nut cluster I could reach with a mesh square and a rubber band. When the birds saw what I had done, they began taking all the nuts I had been unable to cover. I was pretty proud of myself until I noticed they had run out of nuts and were now cutting off entire clusters—cover and all—and flapping with the heavy load up into the nearest spruce to pick it apart. They got them all.

The next year I covered the clusters with duct tape with the same result. My mother, who was in a wheelchair, was living with us then. I briefly considered parking her on the front porch with a .22 rifle to blaze away at the birds, but decided instead to learn to like blue jays. If I had made the effort to cover some or all of the hedge with bird netting I could probably have saved at least some of the crop, but it would have been a nasty job.

Other tree nuts that you could grow in Nova Scotia might be beech, ginkgo, almonds, or pine nuts. The beech is a large forest tree that produces small, highly-flavoured, triangular nuts that are mostly valuable for wildlife. A hundred years ago, the native beech, *Fagus grandifolia*, was one of the most important and useful trees in the Acadian Forest. Not only did it produce nuts, but it was a source of beautiful, rot-resistant lumber. Today it is afflicted with an imported bark disease that has nearly wiped it out.

The European beech (*Fagus sylvatica*) is very similar and appears to be resistant to the bark disease. It probably brought it here in the first place. It is a green tree but is often sold in garden centres as a copper or purple-coloured cultivar. Any European beech seems to be at home in Nova Scotia and can grow into an impressively beautiful tree. The green one at least, and maybe some of the purple ones, produce good crops of nuts.

The ginkgo could be the oldest surviving tree species on earth. Fossilized ginkgo leaves are found with dinosaur bones. The leaf is an interesting fan shape that frequently appears in jewellery design. You would recognize it if you saw it. It is actually more closely related to conifers than it is to the broad-leafed trees.

For centuries the ginkgo tree was thought to be extinct but was discovered still surviving around Chinese temples. Because it was so ancient, it had outlasted all its enemies and was an exceedingly trouble-free tree. It is quite tolerant of air pollution and up to the present day is propagated and planted as a street tree in large cities. It also produces nuts that are popular in the Orient.

Gingko trees are either male or female. The female produces the fruit with the nut inside, but of course, it takes two to tango. Only male trees are propagated and used as street trees because fruits from female trees litter the ground and are slimy and said to smell like vomit.

The almond is a small tree related to the apricot. An apricot pit looks like an almond, and some apricot trees actually have a sweet nut that tastes like an almond. Most apricot seeds, though, are bitter and poisonous with cyanide.

One year at the garden centre, we had a bundle of trees called Hall's Hardy almond. I remember that the leafless trees had a delicious smell. We all planted one but none of them survived. Of course, in those days peaches didn't survive either. Today, peaches are doing well here. Maybe it is time to try almonds again.

Nut-bearing pine trees should do well in Nova Scotia, and the nuts are delicious. The Korean pine (*Pinus Koraiensis*) and the Swiss stone pine (*Pinus cembra*) are hardy and produce good-sized nuts.

If you plant pines for nuts, be sure to plant two for pollination. Many years ago I started some piñon pine trees from nuts my brother sent from New Mexico. I really didn't expect them to survive in Nova Scotia, and in the end I only planted one of them on my property. That tree flourished and grew larger than any piñon I ever saw in New Mexico. Eventually it produced many cones every year, but they were empty. No pollinator.

Finally, the chestnut tree might be worth a try. It is a big, extremely beautiful tree related to the beech. The American chestnut (*Castanea dentata*), was once the king of the forest in eastern

North America, though I don't think it was native to Nova Scotia. It is plenty hardy, though, and could be grown here except that it is practically extinct. It is another victim of an imported disease--the chestnut blight. It was a priceless source of lumber and the fabled chestnuts roasting on an open fire. Today it survives only as ever-weakening sprouts from dying trees.

The Chinese chestnut, (*Castanea mollissima*), is a good-looking apple-tree-sized tree that also produces the tasty chestnut for roasting and is blight-resistant. It might succeed in the very-most-favoured parts of Nova Scotia, but is definitely borderline hardy.

Growing nut trees from nuts is both easy and exciting. If you can get any ripe ones, you can start hazels in pots and transplant them later. The large nut trees don't like to be transplanted and are better started in place.

All nuts are planted in the Fall and have to spend the winter outside, either in the pot or in the ground, in order to germinate in the Spring. If you are planting in place, pick a spot where the tree has room to grow to a ripe old age.

Take off the sod and make a nice, loose, fertile planting spot. You will probably have to remove the husk that covers the seed to find the nut inside. If it is a black walnut, wear gloves or your hands will be stained black for months. Once you have uncovered the nut, plant it two or three inches deep in your prepared spot. Tamp the soil down. It is a good idea to put a piece of wire mesh over it, firmly weighted down, to deter mice and squirrels. Cover the bare ground with a mulch like bark chips or old hay or even evergreen boughs.

Remove the mesh in the Spring so the tree doesn't grow through it. You will be surprised how fast the seedling grows if you keep the grass away from it and don't run over it with the lawn mower.

Since coming to Nova Scotia in 1973, I have tried almost every kind of nut tree. The big ones—even if they grow well—take many years to begin producing, and we sold our place before any had started. The hazels produced right away, but I told you about the problems I had with them.

Now, at my age, I need a small tree that grows quickly and bears early. I am looking for a peanut tree if I can find one.

Bruce Partridge

Small fruits

A big section of the yard at Pleasant Valley Nurseries, alongside and in front of the racks of fruit trees, was devoted to the small fruits. Most customers, even if they didn't plan to try fruit trees, took a good look at these gems. The most popular—with the exception of the strawberries and raspberries, which were sold in bundles out of the cold storage—were the gooseberries, currants, grapes, highbush and lowbush blueberries, and, lately, the haskaps. We also sold elderberries, hardy kiwis, blackberries, josta berries, sometimes highbush cranberry or saskatoon, and oddities such as goji berry. Small fruits were dependable, grew quickly, delivered big crops of berries every Summer, and, in general, had fewer problems than fruit trees.

The gooseberry and currant varieties we are familiar with probably came over on the boats with the first European immigrants to Nova Scotia. They were grown here way before Pleasant Valley Nurseries got started. In the tall grass around an abandoned farm house it was not uncommon to find a patch of red or black currant that had outlived the farm. Currants and gooseberries are working-class berries and should be in every yard.

The fruit of red and black currants are very different, but the plants look almost identical and are hard to tell apart. The best way to sort them out if they get mixed up at the garden centre is by the smell. The twigs and leaves of the black currant have a distinctive musky smell that is easy to detect. The fruit of the black currant also has the musky smell and is not very appetizing to eat raw, but has a solid reputation for jam and certain alcoholic beverages. The red currant, by contrast, is quite tasty raw and also good cooked in cookies and muffins. I like to eat them freshly picked by the handful. They look like a handful of rubies and make a delicious jelly with that same ruby colour.

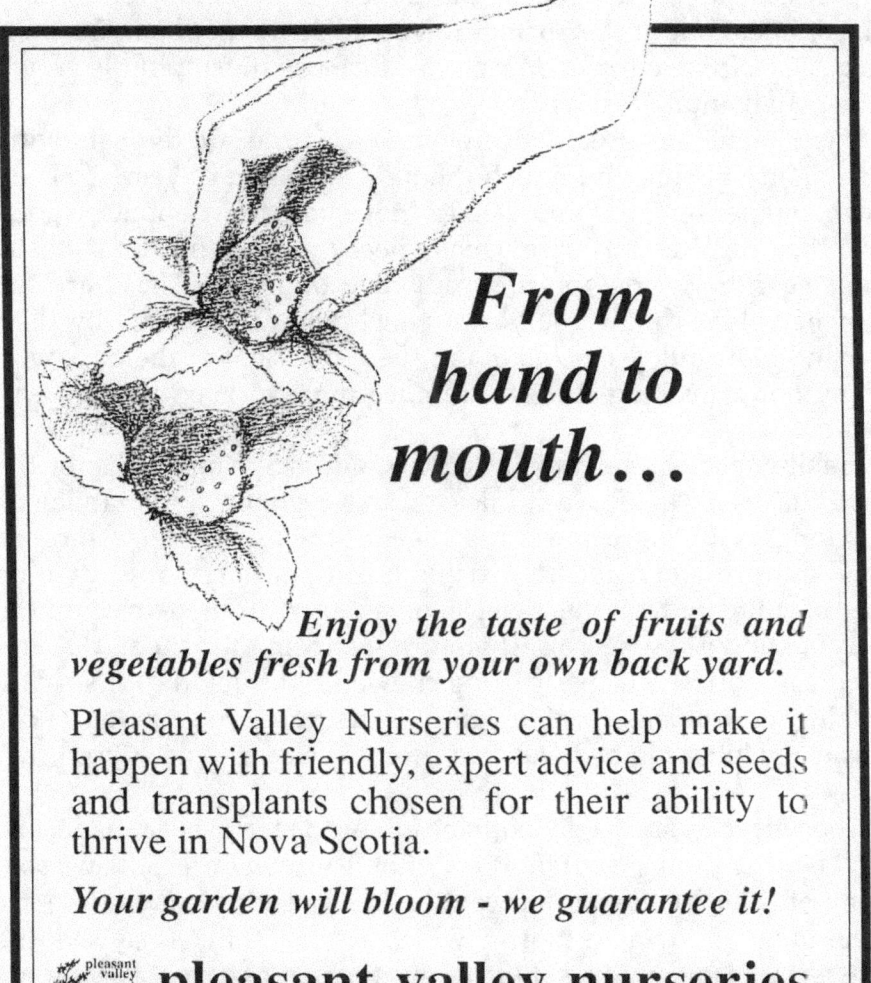

Both the red and black currants grow into a bush about four feet high and are loaded with dangling bunches of berries in mid-summer. Bushes are full-grown in about three years and the amount of fruit they produce is hard to believe. The foliage is bright green, somewhat maple-leaf shaped, and the currants are one of the first things to leaf out in the Spring. You could grow them just for their looks. The alpine currant doesn't produce useful fruit but is grown as an ornamental.

If you plant currants in nicely-worked, fertile soil to begin with, with plenty of sun, and mulch them for a couple of years to keep down competing grass and weeds, they should just about be good for a lifetime. The only care usually necessary is a pruning, ideally every year, to remove old unproductive branches. These are the branches older than three years, which you can identify by their size and their dull grey colour. Cut them out right at the base with loppers or a pruning saw and remove them to keep new growth coming.

Finally, shortly after the bushes leaf out in Spring, watch for the sawfly larvae. These are hordes of active grey worms, about an inch long, that congregate at the edges of the leaves. They start out small but grow fast and can strip a bush in a hurry. You wake up one morning and wonder what happened to all the leaves on the currants and gooseberries. If you are watching for them, the first thing you notice is leaves getting chewed right down to their ribs, usually near the base of the plant. At this stage, you can locate the larvae and kill them by hand, but later it is easier to use pyrethrum spray.

Gooseberries are wildly popular in Europe for pies and jams and maybe other things, but not as commonly grown here. Still, we sold many of them at the garden centre. The varieties grown here are sometimes annoyingly thorny, which I don't think is always the case with European ones, but the fruit is just as nice. Everything I said about currants applies to the gooseberry, including the sawfly.

Incidentally, my brother-in-law in Cape Breton says that when he was a boy, they picked quantities of wild gooseberries from the edges of pastures and woods. Linda Petite once brought me cuttings of wild gooseberries she found on an island in the Bras d'or lakes, which I rooted and grew. The fruits on these bushes were smaller than the cultivated berries—which is usually the case—but tasty.

Grape cultivation in this area was tentative and experimental when Pleasant Valley Nurseries started. There were a couple of big grape vines around the county but we didn't know what variety they were or where they came from. One covered the side of a building at St. Augustine's Monastery in the community of Monastery. Some of these monks came from Europe, and others from the U.S.A. and either may have brought the plants with them. I never had the chance to taste the grapes, but they looked big and juicy.

Quite early on at the garden centre, we were selling grapes which were the Concord type with thick skins that people mostly use for jelly. Our true opinion was that grapes really weren't suited here but might be tried like a peach tree in a protected location.

Everything changed soon after that, when Roger Dial proved that grapes could be grown commercially in the Annapolis Valley, and opened the Grand Pre Winery. Growing wine grapes in Nova Scotia was something we didn't think was possible. Wine grapes were grown in warm places like France or Italy or California. Nevertheless, we paid attention and found out that Roger Dial's first success was with hardy grapes he had imported from Russia. We thought this must be the secret and ordered pots of Michurinetz and Severngy. I planted some at home and they did grow well and are still there today.

Soon, grape growing was taking off and there were wineries starting up from the Annapolis Valley through to Cape Breton, and more varieties of grapes were coming into cultivation. The Michurinetz and Severngy passed into oblivion and were replaced with more blue-blooded wine grapes such as Marechal Foch and Pinot Noir. Customers at the garden centre were very excited about growing grapes and soon we were selling maybe a dozen varieties of wine grapes and table grapes of various names and colours.

No one was talking of climate change yet, but there must have been something happening. Tender plants were starting to survive the winter. Even peaches and weeping mulberries and Japanese maples were doing well. People were having good luck with their grape vines and there was more and more demand. Customers were becoming very knowledgeable about grape culture and were teaching us.

By the time Pleasant Valley Nurseries closed in 2017, there were a good number of grape growers right here in Antigonish County. Kingsley Brown in South Side Harbour was the first to get into it big and show us that it could be done. His example and his help soon got other growers started.

The grape, like the currant, is a very long-lived plant, and needs to be planted well in order to be productive for a long time. Remove the sod all along the row where the grapes will go, in a strip two to three feet wide. Work the soil in this strip well with fertilizer, limestone and lots of organic matter to keep the vines growing vigorously for a long time. Vines are usually kept continuously mulched with organic mulches to keep out competing grass and weeds.

Unlike currants, the site you choose for growing grapes is of paramount importance. The ideal site for a large planting of grapes would be a sunny hillside sloping down to a large body of water, which around here are bays and estuaries of the Northumberland Strait. The vines are thereby protected from the north winds in the winter, while the sloping site ensures that cold air at night keeps drifting downhill and doesn't collect to freeze the vines. A large expanse of water below keeps air a little bit warmer in the Fall and extends the growing season. It also acts to dampen temperature swings from one extreme to another. A homeowner who is only planting a few vines and doesn't have an ocean on his doorstep can do just fine by planting on the south side of buildings or in the sun behind evergreens or a fence.

Serious grape growers train their vines on wires and prune each year to produce new fruiting wood. There are books and manuals on this subject and information on the internet. I never bothered to learn the exact details since I like my grapes growing over a framework that I can sit under in the Summertime. Grapes grown on the wires are undoubtedly larger and sweeter than mine, but I only eat a few and don't make wine from them anyway. I make my wine from elderberries, which are easier to grow.

Highbush blueberries are another relative newcomer to the small fruit scene in this area. Wild or lowbush blueberries grow enthusiastically around here on poor acid soil and worn-out farms, and were being tended and harvested as a commercial crop before we even started Pleasant Valley Nurseries. Our introduction to highbush blueberries was the plastic boxes of huge, tasteless berries in the grocery store. We knew that some growers were cultivating them in the Annapolis Valley, but they were barely hardy and here in the land of wild berries, who needed them?

Customers began asking for them, though, so we brought in a few potted bushes to sell. We were surprised when unsold plants in their pots produced large crops of berries which, eaten straight off the bush, were delicious. We were convinced, but there was still the problem of hardiness here in zone 5b.

Again, the climate must have been changing. Customers were buying the blueberries and coming back for more. We sold all we could get. The highbush blueberry is a desirable plant. Even without berries it is a good-looking plant. The flowers are pretty, the leaves are glossy, and the Fall colour is outstanding. It can go right in front of the house.

The highbush blueberry does need a lot of sun, and doesn't do well if the soil dries out. Keep the soil around the bushes mulched. Mulch holds moisture in the soil and also discourages competing grasses and weeds—another thing with which blueberries can't cope. For best fruiting, plant bushes four to six feet apart in beds of prepared soil as if for grapes. The difference is that, unlike grapes and all other fruit crops that I am aware of, the blueberry actually requires an acid soil. This means that you don't add any limestone to the soil. Thanks to acid rain, our soil in Nova Scotia is generally acidic anyway.

The blueberry is a curious plant that absolutely requires good drainage but not an exceptionally high level of soil fertility. Rotted manure or leaves, compost and bone meal are good soil amendments for blueberries. Peat moss works well to loosen the soil and keep it that way, improving drainage, while at the same time storing moisture. It also acidifies the soil. If possible, plant in raised beds that guarantee good drainage, then mulch well.

Since maybe the last ten years or so, there has been a strong push to establish the haskap—a berry-producing type of honeysuckle—as a commercial crop in Nova Scotia. The companies growing and selling the plants promote the haskap as hardier than the highbush blueberry, with fruit earlier and higher in nutrition and antioxidants. For a while it was something of a craze. Haskap culture was promoted at public meetings that painted a bright picture of the money to be made selling berries both here and in the orient. Thousands of plants were sold commercially. In some cases, hopeful citizens who had never grown anything in their lives bought hundreds of plants to start plantations. Some of these plantations must have been successful and now it is possible to find haskap juice and jelly in the store, but I think the explosion of popularity has yet to take off.

In my last years at the garden centre, we sold a good quantity of potted haskaps. Pollination requirements were confusing. It seemed like the best pollinator was a strain that had good pollen but bad berries. The plants were attractive and vigorous, though the feedback we got from customers was a bit on the negative side. The plants did grow to a respectable size—six or seven feet in ordinary garden soil—and bore large crops of berries, but these dropped off if not harvested in time. Several customers told us that they had never tasted a berry because the birds took them all before they were ripe.

There is a good chance that I am not giving this berry the credit it deserves because I have never grown it, so I will leave it at that. What interests me is that a wild haskap actually grows here in Nova Scotia, mostly around the Atlantic shore. Scientifically it is *Lonicera caerulea*, the Mountain fly-honeysuckle. I once rooted cuttings from a few of these and grew them in my garden. They were quite variable in form and did produce sweet berries, but not surprisingly, these were much smaller than cultivated haskaps.

Borderline Hardy in 5b

When our kids were growing up and we lived on the farm, we grew or attempted to grow every kind of berry possible. Now our kids are grown and we've sold the farm and we like to spend our time at our cabin in Cape Breton. The cabin is surrounded by wild fruit. Starting with serviceberries and wild strawberries, the raspberries, blackberries, blueberries, cranberries, elderberries, chokecherries, chokeberries and rose hips ripen as the season progresses. Not every type is good every year, however. In the wild, a bumper crop one year often means no crop the next. Nevertheless, something is good every summer. Rose hips never fail. We like to get out picking.

You can grow many of these wild berries at home, and we tried most of them. Serviceberries, elderberries and chokeberries are easy to grow and are highly ornamental as well. One wouldn't ordinarily grow chokecherry, of which there are more than enough in the wild. The same goes for the blackberry. The wild rose is ubiquitous and a prolific producer, and doesn't need our help. Now that I have time, I like to let nature grow the fruit so I can pick it from the wild—except for a couple of things.

One wild fruit that I feel is well worth growing at home is the elderberry. As I said, it is attractive, with lush foliage and large white flower clusters which are themselves edible. The kicker is that the research station in Kentville has developed some strains of elderberry that are hugely more productive than the wild ones. These have names like Nova, York, Victoria, and Scotia, and produce fruit clusters so heavy that they bend the branches down and break them. The individual berries are almost as large as blueberries. At one time I made a lot of wine and these elderberry varieties were the perfect thing. They were very quick to pick and made first class wine. I never felt the need to fuss with grapes.

Two other fruits that can be picked in the wild and which I have glossed over are the strawberry and the raspberry. Both of these, I would say, should be, and usually are, cultivated at home. The wild strawberry is a far cry from the cultivated one with which we are so familiar. The wild one may be sweeter but it is so tiny. Not to mention that the mosquitoes and black flies are at their worst just as they ripen. I admire anyone who does a serious picking of wild strawberries. Wild raspberries can be good, and sometimes almost as large as cultivated ones, but they are very unpredictable. It is hard to find a patch that produces well every year. The dry summers we have been having for the last couple of years seem to spoil the crop. You can mulch a planting at home. and water it if necessary, and it should produce well for years.

Cultivated strawberries are often the first fruit a budding home gardener attempts. They are adaptable and can grow in the garden or in flower beds or even planters and pots. There are main crop varieties that bear a heavy crop all at once, or ever-bearing varieties that bear steadily through the summer. All produce the big berries we are familiar with.

Strawberries appreciate a reasonably loose and fertile soil—just like you would prepare for any crop—worked up with organic matter, and maybe peat moss and a bit of limestone. They need lots of sun. If you can put them in where you have grown something before, the soil is probably good and the weeds under control. Strawberry plants also can go in sunny flower beds, pots and planters.

Weeds and grass are the biggest enemies of strawberries. When preparing the soil, take out all the weeds and roots that you can find. Plant strawberry plants about a foot and a half apart down the row. They should be in a bed at least two feet wide; through the summer the bed will fill in with new plants produced by runners from the mother plant. Pick off any flowers that appear on the mother plant so its energy goes into producing runners. The next summer you get the big harvest of berries from all the plants that have filled in the bed.

Keep grass and weeds in check by diligent weeding or else by mulching. After the first plants are set, mulch them with a layer of straw, or old hay, grass clippings, even bark mulch or wood shavings to discourage weeds. The mulch also keeps moisture in the soil and limits temperature fluctuation. When using mulch, it is necessary to clear a spot for the little plants at the ends of the runners so that they can root in the soil. Put them where you want them and place a little rock to hold them down while they root.

About six rooted runners from each plant should fill up the bed. Cover strawberry plantings with straw or evergreen boughs, or both, for the winter.

Raspberries also do best in a nicely-worked, fertile soil. Set one-year-old canes in the ground four or five inches deep and about two feet apart. Through the summer, new canes will shoot up from the original ones to fill up those two-foot gaps and make a solid row. All these new canes will have berries next summer. Before winter, tie the raspberry canes to a wire strung between two stakes, or in bunches to stakes driven along the row, to prevent snow and wind breaking the canes. A heavy mulch alongside the plants is good any time of year, and is especially important before winter.

Unlike strawberries, a planting of which is good at best for two or three years, you can maintain a planting of raspberries for a decade, at least. This, though, requires some diligence. Grass and weeds are always trying to get in, the soil fertility tries to run out, and the raspberries try to escape from the row. This means weeding or mulching, fertilizing, and driving a spade into the soil to cut off raspberry sprouts that are growing out of bounds into the path. Annual pruning of the canes in the row is also necessary to keep it producing. After the picking is done, cut out all the canes that had berries right at the base, leaving the straight, unbranched ones that are just growing and will produce the berries next year.

If all this gets ahead of you and, as often happens, you end up with a raspberry thicket, don't feel bad—you aren't alone, and you'll still be able to crawl in and get a lot of berries.

Bruce Partridge

Site selection

Selecting an appropriate site for plantings, or appropriate plantings for a site, requires some thought. You must consider the conditions of wind and sun, soil, proximity to buildings or roads or salt water, types of plants desired, degree of maintenance, and other factors. You can ignore many of these things in the case of a tough shrub or perennial, but they may be crucial for a large tree, an expensive planting, or a borderline hardy plant.

At the garden centre, no matter what people were planting, the first questions I always asked were:

- Is the spot sunny or shady?
- Which way does it face?
- How much sun does it get during the day?

You can change the soil or certain other things to suit the plant, but you can't change the sun. The most popular flowering plants at the garden centre tend to want as much sun as they can get. If the site is shady, this narrows down the choice considerably. Plants that like the sun might survive in the shade, but they will never look good. It may be a matter of choosing a rhododendron or hydrangea instead of a rose.

If shade is too deep, or there is no direct sun at all, the spot may be suitable only for ferns and certain perennials such as Bergenia or Hosta. If a building casts shade, there probably isn't much you can do about it. If it is due to trees, you might be able to thin out and remove branches to let in more sun. Some wildflowers and early-blooming bulbs are actually adapted to grow and bloom in the Spring sun beneath trees that haven't leafed out yet.

The next most important question is that of exposure. Is the site sloping or flat? Is it windy or sheltered? Is it close to buildings? Is it close to the seashore or a salted highway? Does the snow build up there in winter? Does the snowplow have room to pile the snow? You can guess the significance of most of these questions.

If the site is sloping, it will be harder to do the soil preparation and planting, though the end result can be very pleasing. A planting bed on a slope should still be constructed higher than the original level to provide better soil fertility and drainage. A sloping site is rarely well-drained—only on top. It might be necessary to build a low retaining wall of wood, brick or stone to hold in the soil. A planting on a flat area is much easier than on a slope but requires a different arrangement of plants to prevent larger plants from hiding smaller ones.

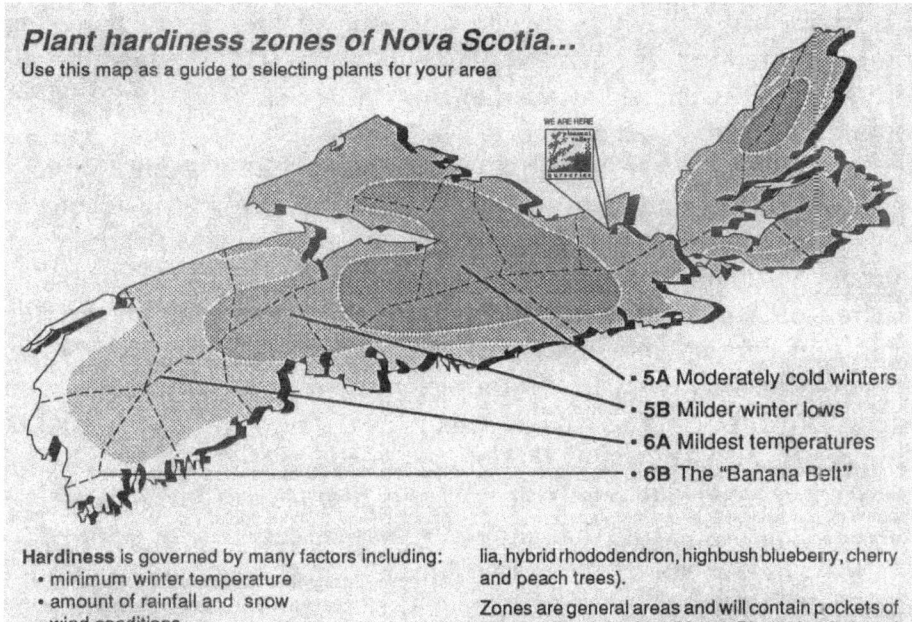

Plant hardiness zones of Nova Scotia...
Use this map as a guide to selecting plants for your area

- 5A Moderately cold winters
- 5B Milder winter lows
- 6A Mildest temperatures
- 6B The "Banana Belt"

Hardiness is governed by many factors including:
- minimum winter temperature
- amount of rainfall and snow
- wind conditions
- average length of frost-free period

Most plants sold by us are hardy in zone **5A**. Some plants are recommended only for zone **5B** (magnolia, hybrid rhododendron, highbush blueberry, cherry and peach trees).

Zones are general areas and will contain pockets of warmer or cooler conditions. Plants in sheltered positions will grow well even in a cooler zone, especially low growing plants which are protected by snow cover in the winter.

If the site is windy and exposed, it is not a good bet for brittle or tender species. If it is sheltered, the opposite is true. It is not easy to provide shelter from the wind. You can plant windbreaks, but they take a few years to start blocking wind and require careful planning so as not to cause snow drifts in the wrong places. It may be possible to take advantage of existing evergreens for shelter. Consider building structures such as fences, arbours, or pergolas to block the wind, but they must be strong and must not cast excessive shade on the planting.

The amount of exposure to the wind—along with the amount of sun—determines, to a great extent, what you can plant. Existing buildings will affect exposure to both wind and sun. The closer the buildings are to the planting, the greater the effect. A house or another sizable building can provide valuable shelter from the wind and, in some cases, the sun. A building facing south or southeast protects from the strong, cold north winds and accepts the sun. A planting here will winter well and come to life early. Flowering bulbs planted in this micro climate will bloom with the first breath of Spring as it chases away the long Nova Scotia winter. Spring-blooming shrubs are good here, too.

You must plan carefully plantings close to the seashore or to a highway that is salted in the winter. Storms blowing in from the sea can carry salt water spray onto plants at any season of the year. Almost any plant is susceptible to damage when salt spray strikes the leaves. Some conifers are resistant, and also certain deciduous plants in winter when they have no leaves. Salt spray also blows from salted highways in winter when traffic whips up salt-laden slush and the wind carries it. This is also very injurious to plants and can be even more deadly than sea spray.

Extensive lists are available of plants that show some salt resistance. The list of plants that show no salt resistance is much longer.

Heavy snow can break or tear limbs from trees and shrubs that are brittle. Burning-bushes and Norway maples come to mind, for a start. If you are planting in a spot where snow always accumulates in winter, take this into account.

Paradoxically, deep snow can be a good thing for some plants. Tender hydrangeas, for instance, are more likely to survive and bloom well next summer if they have spent the winter buried by snow. The same thing could be the case with broadleaf evergreens that tend to have their leaves burned by wind and sun in the winter. Hollies don't break or burn and come through the winter in perfect condition after being buried by snow.

Rhododendrons are brittle and can break, but that is not always a bad thing. I remember one winter when deep snow froze to the branches of everyone's rhododendrons, then subsided—breaking the branches as it went down. It looked like a major disaster but it wasn't. The branches, in most cases, hadn't broken completely off. They only cracked and drooped until they were resting on the ground. They healed in that position and the plant mounded up from there, as it grew. Broken rhododendrons even looked better than before and could never break again because their branches rested on the ground.

On the subject of snow, don't forget the snowplow. The operator will need somewhere to push the snow—not right over your planting, we hope.

The third consideration must be the soil. Only the third because you can often amend or modify soil to suit the plants. The most obvious question to ask is whether the area is wet or dry. If the customer says, "Wet," you can bet it is.

No tree or shrub will do well plunged into wet ground. A planting hole dug into wet ground—even if filled with excellent soil—quickly becomes a waterlogged pit useless for planting. Even the weeping willow, which is universally known to like water, won't succeed in a hole like this. The roots quickly suffocate and rot. You must start trees and shrubs planted in wet areas in natural or man-made mounds above the grade. Here they can get a good start and gather momentum before they begin to root into the wet ground.

Homeowners often have wet ground, but think it is dry. The wettest time of year is the Spring, when the snow is melting and the rain is coming down. This is when back yards and low-lying land are waterlogged and trees die. The same area may be nice and dry a couple of months later, when out comes the barbecue and badminton net, but the damage has been done. Again, you can grow trees and shrubs in a situation like this by planting in raised beds and mounds above the general level of the ground.

Dry ground is a rarer occurrence in this area and may take different forms. I am relieved when I hear that the ground is "dry", because that usually, but not always, implies that the drainage is good and plants will not drown. Exceptions can be banks that are bulldozed down to rock-hard subsoil and are dry because water runs off, or areas where buildings prevent rain from reaching the soil. It can be dry where large trees suck up all the water and is almost always dry in summer under heavy sod.

You can improve dry soil that is well-drained to be very productive ground by incorporating plenty of organic matter such as manure or compost and peat moss. Organic matter decomposes into humus, which clogs up the larger pores in the soil, slowing drainage, improving water-holding capacity, and adding fertility. Trees and shrubs root deeply in well-drained ground and can be exceptionally strong, wind-firm and long-lived. Orchards on well-drained ground can be very productive. Sometimes trees root deeply enough to reach the water table, where there is always water. The best-looking weeping willows that I know of are on gravelly river intervals where they have rooted down to the water table.

Soil can also be classified as "natural" or as "disturbed". Soil around houses or buildings, drives and roadways constructed since the invention of the bulldozer is almost sure to be disturbed. It would have been turned upside down during excavation of the basement, the subsoil piled on top, pushed around—usually soaking wet—sculpted and packed down with heavy machinery. The result, once dry, is more like pavement than soil. With a few inches of topsoil, you might be able to grow grass, but the only way to successfully grow shrubs and trees in this situation will be generous raised beds of fertile soil built on top of the disturbed ground.

Theoretically, now that most basements are dug with an excavator, subsoil can be trucked away and natural soil around the construction site may be less disturbed. It is still common to see excavation taking place in wet weather, however, with vehicles stuck and the ground churned into a quagmire. Landscaping won't be easy around these places. Besides construction upheaval, any compacted or polluted soil can be considered disturbed. Even farm fields may be compacted by heavy machinery or poisoned by improper use of fertilizer or pesticides.

Natural soil is a gift for the landscaper and gardener. It is soil that has developed beneath natural vegetation, or is found around old farmhouses, or in former gardens or even fields that have always been in pasture. Unless it is in a bog or a rock quarry, the soil is probably workable and has at least a little fertility. Plantings are straightforward: simply remove the sod, turn the soil, and fertilize. Raising the area with additional soil makes the planting look better and can do no harm, but probably isn't necessary.

If you are blessed with natural soil—keep it that way. We often saw properties where all the natural vegetation, including the soil, had been bulldozed off to make way for grass or some unrealistic dream of imported fruit trees or towering maples. It might take another ice age for these areas to recover.

Finally, assessing an area for planting, one must watch for physical obstacles, competing vegetation or predatory animals. Physical obstacles might be overhead or underground wires, or pipes. Rock outcroppings might be incorporated as a feature.

Large established trees such as maple, ash or oak tie up the soil underneath with a mass of roots. They immediately suck up any water or nutrients. The trees also block the sun. It is usually a waste of time to try to plant anything other than ferns and perennials under big trees. Heavy sod and aggressive weeds also threaten plantings. You must remove the sod and keep it well away. Deep mulches combat both sod and weeds.

Predatory animals include mice, rabbits, deer and wandering domestic animals, including dogs—yours and your neighbours. Any and all of these can ruin a planting. Where trouble is expected or suspected, you can take measures to defend against the smaller animals. Larger ones might have to be fenced out, though there are now effective deer repellents available where garden supplies are sold.

Bruce Partridge

Flowering shrubs

The first Spring that I began working at PVN—1978—was an exciting time. Henri had hired me on to mow lawns with Pete Stovell. Henri and Frank had landed what seemed like a lucrative contract mowing the grass around the buildings and houses of the Michelin Tire plant in New Glasgow, and other contracts around Antigonish town. This kept Pete and me going steady unless it was raining—which it seemed to do several days a week in those years.

At the garden centre, the trees and shrubs were already planted out in the field in rows. Very few shrubs came in pots in those days, so we either potted them ourselves or planted them out in the field. I enjoyed showing up for work a few minutes early and wandering through the shrubs with my *Encyclopedia of Canadian Gardening,* trying to figure out how to tell one from another.

Roscoe Fillmore, an old-time nurseryman from the Annapolis Valley, wrote the Encyclopedia, and it contained all sorts of fascinating information about the shrubs, including how to propagate them.

Flowering shrubs, at that time, were what you could call old-fashioned. They were primarily big, tough species brought by colonists from the old countries—the lilacs, honeysuckles, mock oranges, viburnums, forsythias, spireas, and hydrangeas, to mention a few. It was common to see an old farm house smothered in these shrubs—most which could reach eight feet or more. The perfume of the lilacs, honeysuckles and mock oranges could knock you out. The only problem was their size.

Even around a very tall house, these shrubs might cover the downstairs windows in a few years, if planted too close. Once it became necessary to start chopping to keep them down, they never looked very good again.

Also, house styles were changing. The one-story bungalows and ranch-styles and split-levels were becoming popular, and there was a demand for lower-growing shrubs to go around them. Very soon, plant breeders were sending out miniature spireas and potentillas, and even dwarf versions of the lilacs, honeysuckles, forsythias, viburnums and mock oranges. Many of these only grew to three or four feet high and were more in keeping with the scale of the modern house. These dwarf flowering shrubs are available now in an almost-infinite variety, and can be very colourful. The golden ones show up for blocks. They do combine well with low evergreens or specimen trees in plantings and are very popular.

Nowadays it can be hard to find the big, old-fashioned shrubs that we used to love. They still can't be beat for a tall shrub border or a hedgerow away from the house, where they can grow as big as they want. They provide roosting and nesting habitat for birds, which fatten on their berries before the winter migration. They are as tough and as fragrant as they were in Roscoe Fillmore's days. Maybe we could start building houses taller again.

At Pleasant Valley Nurseries, in summer, there was no need of a calendar to tell which month it was. The flowering shrubs told us. First it was the month of forsythia, quince, service berry, the early rhododendrons and magnolias, and the Garland spirea.

Bruce Partridge

Forsythia.

Giddy with the flowers and the first lovely days of summer, as were we all, early gardeners shopped for seeds and supplies, maybe a tree or one of those shrubs. Business picked up and the stage was set for the explosion—the month of the lilac, the crab apple, the honeysuckle, the white spireas, the weigela, the viburnum, the mock orange, the big rhododendrons and the azaleas...and a parking lot jammed with gardeners. School ended, and children arriving with their parents picked up flowers from the paths to throw in the pond.

With the summer heat, things slowed and it was the month of the rose, the Chinese dogwood, the red spireas, and the little potentilla. At the garden centre and nursery, it was the month of fertilizing and repotting, pruning, spacing, re-arranging, and lots and lots of watering. It was the month of catching up.

When the first hydrangeas came into bloom, we knew it would soon be the month of the Fall Sale, and cooler weather. The burning bushes began to burn with crimson, and many of the shrubs that had bloomed earlier now sported clusters of colourful berries.

Bruce Partridge

All the hydrangeas were soon blooming, as well as the Rose of Sharon. There would be a last flurry of sales and then time to put things away for the winter.

At last, as we shut up the store and disbanded until Spring, the witch-hazel was blooming.

Evergreens

The popularity of evergreens in the landscape goes up and down like the stock market. When Pleasant Valley Nurseries was starting in the 70s, popularity was high. It seemed that evergreens were what everyone wanted. Most old houses, if there were any plantings at all, featured an old-fashioned lilac or a Hansa rose, and a few seriously overgrown cedars or yews. There were few people at that time who were keenly motivated to plant ornamentals around their homes. I think the prevailing attitude was to put some green things by the corners and beside the step and be done with it.

At first, we were okay with that and were happy to be selling cedars and yews. Soon enough, though, we became aware of the almost limitless variety of evergreens grown elsewhere, and their potential uses in the landscape. Conifers, or needle leaf evergreens, included cedar, juniper, yew, false cypress, spruce and pine, and a few lesser-known species. You could get them large or small, from forest-sized trees to dwarfs less than a foot high. They came in every shade of green, of blue-green, of blue, of silver, of copper and of gold.

At PVN, we began to bring in a modest selection of what was available, and were beginning to grow some of the nicer ones at the nursery in Lakevale. The Agriculture College in Truro had a respectable evergreen collection and was a good place to take cuttings. The variety of shapes and sizes and colours available in evergreens was so extensive that it would have been possible to do an entire residential planting of evergreens if anyone could afford it.

Evergreens are somewhat expensive, however. This is no mystery when you consider that it takes anywhere from five to ten years to grow a saleable-sized evergreen, compared to one or two for a flowering shrub. Fortunately, they do combine nicely with flowering shrubs and perennials and are generally not planted in masses except on government jobs.

Gardeners coming to shop at PVN became steadily more discriminating as the years went by, and eventually the sales of evergreens levelled off. Customers still bought choice specimens to combine with flowering shrubs and perennials in their plantings, or to showcase in selected spots in a rock garden, but few were buying the big yews and pyramid cedars anymore. Sales of large-growing evergreen trees like blue spruce and Austrian pine never fell off, though, and even increased over the years. Sometimes we brought in evergreen trees as big as we could handle and they sold despite the price.

We at Pleasant Valley Nurseries were as excited as anyone at the glowing new varieties of evergreens coming in from Ontario each year, and we planted many of them at our own homes. Some of them were almost irresistible to customers as well, and we were eager to sell them and see how they would do. This we did, though, with some trepidation.

It was important to find out just where the customer intended to plant them: how much or how little sun did the site get, how much wind, how much snow, what the soil was like, etc. A customer doesn't want to pay for an expensive evergreen and see it die, and neither did we. We gave the best advice we could and sometimes discouraged planting where we guessed chances were poor. We didn't want to see those evergreens come back half burnt by the wind, or dead.

I always felt most confident selling dwarf spruce and pine, and almost as confident selling yew and false cypress. I seldom saw these injured by the sun or the wind or the snow. Upright cedars and junipers were more nerve-wracking. They could look wonderful in the right spot and right soil, but in the wrong spot they were prone to burn during the winter and come out in Spring looking pretty brown.. They could grow out of this and look good again if it only happened once, but this was small comfort to a disappointed customer.

We recommended spruces, pines and junipers for sunny locations—not too windy for junipers, please. The Austrian pine and native white spruce are handsome and tough and can't be beat for planting in exposed locations or next to the seashore. Norway spruce requires more shelter but has an attractive drooping habit. All three grow to an impressively large size.

Mary edging evergreens.

The people's favourite—the Colorado blue spruce—is not quite as happy here but usually does well. The dwarf mugho pine and the dwarf cultivars of the white, Norway and Colorado blue spruces are wonderful in rock gardens and mixed plantings. They are slow-growing, attractive and tough. The dwarf Alberta Spruce is a slow-growing, conical selection of the native white spruce, and is tough and dependable—even in the shade. Spreading junipers come in all shapes and sizes and a wide range of colours. They also can be very good in sunny plantings where there is not too much wind.

Cedars and false cypress can handle some shade—not too windy for cedars, please. The threadleaf false cypress is a very hardy evergreen and can do well in full sun or part shade. Dwarf threadleaf false cypresses are good, slow-growing plants. Some are a glowing gold in colour. There are other species of false cypress that are upright and blue or gold, and unremarkable, except for the Nootka false cypress. This one is native to the Northwest coast of Canada and the U.S.A., where it grows into a towering tree a hundred feet tall. In small sizes it has a rich green colour and gracefully drooping branches. Here on the East coast, it grows slowly and never gets over about twenty feet high, but has proven to be surprisingly hardy and dependable.

Yews are a good choice for shade, but can handle almost anything except deer, including full sun. Most are cultivars of the Japanese yew and tend to grow big and blocky. They can be clipped into any shape or size, including free form animals or birds if you like, or hedges.

All evergreens need good drainage which means planting them in raised beds just to be safe.

Broadleaf evergreens

The spruces and pines, cedars and junipers and false cypress and yews are all needleleaf evergreens or conifers. Everyone is familiar with the needles of the spruce and pine. These are its leaves. Another type of evergreen is the broadleaf evergreen. As the name implies, the leaves are wide and usually long, and stay green all winter. By and large, besides being evergreen, they are known for their spectacular flowers in Spring.

Broadleaf evergreens, with few exceptions, are members of the blueberry family—the Ericaceae. The most popular of these are the rhododendrons and azaleas, which grow in an almost infinite variety of sizes and flower colours. Not a large percentage are hardy in Nova Scotia but just a little piece of infinity is a big number. We have plenty to choose from.

All members of the blueberry family require acidic soil, which is not the common situation in horticulture. Most other plants do best in soil that is close to neutral in acidity. Not all the members of the blueberry family are evergreen like the rhododendron, either. The blueberry itself loses its leaves in the winter. The azalea is a rhododendron that loses its leaves. Botanically, an azalea and a rhododendron are identical, and we lump them together as broadleaf "evergreens" in the genus *Rhododendron*.

Rhododendron at Willow Garden.

Soil in Nova Scotia is almost always acidic and naturally suited to rhododendrons. Often all that you need when planting them are peat moss to improve drainage and bone meal or compost or a bit of granular fertilizer for nutrients. Fertilizer companies sell a wide variety of fertilizers for rhododendrons and azaleas and they probably are all good if you don't overdo them. Captain Steele, a rhododendron grower from the South shore—sadly deceased—,when asked what sort of fertilizer to use on rhododendrons replied, "Whatever you would use on potatoes." This probably meant 6-12-12 farm fertilizer that comes in big bags.

Other cultivated flowering evergreens in the blueberry family include the heathers, wintergreen, pieris, kalmia, and bearberry, to name a few. The highbush blueberry itself is a choice ornamental.

Some widely planted broadleaf evergreens are not in the blueberry family. These include the hollies, mahonias, euonymus and boxwood.

I have travelled around most parts of North America at one time or another, and can say that I've never seen evergreens doing as well as they do in Nova Scotia—especially the dwarfs. Other parts of the continent are too hot, or too cold, or too dry. Where it is too hot or too dry, plants grow too fast or look dusty and burned by the heat. Where it is too cold, they just don't grow.

We have the perfect climate here for many evergreens. They love our cool summers (even if we don't) and our rain and fog. Our soil is not too rich (an understatement). All this combines to keep dwarfs tight and compact, which is how they should be. Our soil has enough in it to keep them rich and green without them growing too fast. I could almost say that dwarf evergreens were invented for Nova Scotia.

The large-growing evergreen trees do well here too, of course. Our native white pine and white spruce are two of the most attractive evergreen trees to be found anywhere. The eastern hemlock can be magnificent, and our balsam fir is the best Christmas tree there is. Soil and climate in Nova Scotia also suit the broadleaf evergreens—the rhododendrons and azaleas and all the other members of the blueberry family. This makes sense when you consider that vast areas of Nova Scotia are covered naturally in blueberry and their relatives.

In Maryvale, Antigonish County, Bill Wilgenhof and his partner Sharon Bryson have demonstrated this in a big way, with extensive plantings of rhododendrons and azaleas, as well as magnolias and other exotics, most propagated in their own facilities—many from seed. A stroll through their Willow Garden in June is an education in the vast variability and beauty of rhododendron species, and something you won't forget. Sadly, Bill passed away recently at the age of 100, taking with him the lifetime of gardening knowledge and wisdom that he so generously shared with us all. Sharon remains a plant expert in her own right. She knows all Bill's tricks and then some, and is more than capable of picking up the slack if she chooses. We wish her all the best.

The choice of evergreens in cultivation is colourful and vast. Hardy evergreens that can grow in Nova Scotia come in all shapes, sizes, and colours, and comprise many different species. When the popularity of evergreens rises again, it should happen here.

Bruce Partridge

Perennials

Strictly speaking, any plant that survives the winters and comes back each Spring is perennial. In the garden centre, though, the word refers to the herbaceous perennials—plants that die down to the ground each Fall and sprout back up in the Spring. Some perennials, such as rhubarb and asparagus, are edible, but the vast majority are grown for the beauty of their flowers and foliage alone.

The selection is vast, and their beauty is unquestionable. A skilled gardener can blend and combine perennials in plantings that take your breath away. There are perennials to suit any situation—wet areas, dry areas, sunny areas, shady areas, and there will be something to grow under any difficult conditions you care to name. Some perennials even require difficult conditions.

Perennials vary hugely in the size to which they grow, in both height and girth. They may be six feet high or six inches—maybe even higher or lower. They may form a narrow clump or spread wide. Some bloom in the Spring, some in the Summer, and some in the Fall. The blooming period of an herbaceous perennial tends to be rather short—a matter of weeks—but during this period they may be smothered in bloom. Most, to make up for the short blooming period, have good-looking leaves, and many—particularly those adapted to the shade and of course the ferns—are planted specifically for their foliage.

As you can see, working with perennials is more complicated than just digging up a piece of ground and filling it with flowers. Not that perennials are difficult to grow, but one must be knowledgeable about how high they are going to grow, when they will bloom, what they will look like in bloom, what their foliage looks like, and what other perennials they combine well with in order to do a planting that will look good all summer. Some perennials are striking enough to stand alone, but most are combined in plantings where each enhances the other. The objective is usually to include species with various blooming times so that something is always in bloom. Take the foliage into account so that plants that are not in bloom still contribute to the composition. Plants should be crowded enough that after a year or two there will be no room for weeds.

Perennials enhance a house.

If all of this sounds daunting, it is not. See what your neighbours are growing. Maybe join the garden club. Get advice at the garden centre. There are numerous good books on the subject and every year a raft of magazine articles. Get a few perennials and plant them: they'll look good right away and you can add to them whenever you want.

Perennials give you back more than your money's worth. They grow fast and after a couple of years you can divide them to use in other plantings, or to trade with friends. They rarely die over winter, and if they aren't doing well you can easily move them to another spot. Perennial gardening is endlessly interesting. There are always new ones to try and new combinations. It is somewhat like vegetable gardening in that you never get everything perfect, but you get a new try every Spring. It can keep you going into a ripe old age.

Preparing a perennial bed is pretty straightforward. The plants don't usually need anything special. You just need to take off the sod over the area you want to plant, then loosen up the soil and mix in organic matter—manure, compost, rotted leaves etc.—to add fertility to the soil and fluff it up. Peat moss is good but there are no nutrients in it so you might want to dig in some granular fertilizer as well. A little of this stuff wouldn't hurt in any case, and some limestone is always good.

When you are digging be sure and search diligently for weed roots and get them out. Weeds are about the only thing that can spoil a perennial planting. Couch grass is the worst and is common. It is identifiable by clumps of fairly tall grass connected with tough, stringy, white underground roots or rhizomes. If it gets in your perennials it wants to take over and is very hard to get rid of. Broadleaf weeds, like dandelions, resemble the perennials and may not be too noticeable in the planting, but couch grass is always unsightly and obvious.

When you are done digging, the loose soil in the bed should be at least six inches deep and mounded up somewhat. If it isn't, add more soil to the bed and work it in. Now plant. Be sure to put some sort of organic mulch around all your plants to keep the soil moist and to keep out those weeds. Shredded bark, old hay, straw, or even grass clippings work well.

You're on your way.

Wildflower gardening

My wife, Mary, and I operated a side business, "Borealis Wildflowers", for quite a few years, growing native wildflowers and selling them through the mail. Inevitably, we planted wildflowers all over our property in Black Avon, and many of them are still there today.

Wildflowers, once planted, tend to find their own niche and hang on to it. In fact, the most interesting and amusing fact we discovered about wildflowers is that if they don't like the spot where you planted them, they will move. More than once, a plant struggled unhappily and died in the spot we had chosen, only to reappear and thrive in a completely different place—even years later.

We had a small farm with a variety of habitats for a wildflower to choose from, ranging from tended bark-mulched shrub beds to rough and snaggly woods. An unexpected colony of wildflowers could appear anywhere, started, I guess, from seeds scattered by our first clumsy planting. These colonies, which had chosen their own spots to grow, invariably thrived and spread. As the years went by, wildflowers actually went wild, intermingling on their own and requiring very little interference from us. That is the essence of wildflower gardening—getting plants started and then letting them go. From time to time, a new wildflower appeared that we didn't remember planting and that must have somehow arrived on its own.

Black-eyed Susan with swamp milkweed.

To be honest, not all of our wildflower plantings were trouble-free. We sold or planted three categories of wildflowers: woodland, wetland and meadow plants. The wetland and meadow plants were largely fast-growing, robust and tough. They could fend for themselves and almost always succeeded in plantings. Woodland plants, on the other hand, were often not so vigorous. In the wild they grow under the leafy trees of the forest where the soil is loose and rich, and the plant community is settled and stable. This was not exactly the case where we planted on our farm. We could duplicate the soil and shade conditions, but the plant community was not at all stable.

Wildflowers had to cope with the tough garden weeds that come with civilization. Mary and I spent plenty of time on our hands and knees, pulling weeds that threatened our delicate woodland pets. One planting in particular featured a hollow log set among trout lily, Dutchman's breeches, hepatica, maidenhair fern and similar treasures. These were happy in this spot, under old apple trees, and were slowly spreading, but needed constant protection.

I had carelessly let Dame's rocket get started and it wanted to grow four feet high and take over. Then there was an annual crop of lamb's quarters and hemp nettle that also wanted to take over. They ran right over our little six-inch woodlanders. It took a lot of weeding each summer to keep them safe.

In areas a little deeper into the woods, though, the weeds weren't bad and wildflowers established themselves without asking our permission. There is no thrill quite like discovering a community of wildflowers in its home in the wild. Unhappily, the wild is threatened on every side. Farming and forestry and housing developments remove forest and plow up land with no let-up. Undisturbed areas of woodland are smaller and smaller every year and harder to find.

The Acadian forest and the wildflower communities that grew up with it are a threatened ecosystem. As I write this, less than 1% of Nova Scotia woodlands remain as old-growth original forest. This 1% is scattered all across the province, mostly in small fragments where rough topography makes it hard to harvest trees.

In my wanderings I found tiny areas of ancient trees and wildflowers. I kept these areas a secret, but in almost every case the trees were cut soon after I discovered them. It was uncanny and sad. These bits of forest and their wildflower communities will take at least a lifetime to recover—if they ever do. A few years ago, Henri Steeghs and I collaborated on a film, *Treasures of the Old Forest*, which touches on Nova Scotia's forests and wildflowers and is available on YouTube.

Shooting star.

Digging wildflowers from the wild is unacceptable, unless the plants are threatened with destruction by some development. If plants are obviously widespread and common it is probably okay to take a couple for your own garden, but not for sale. At Borealis Wildflowers we started all our plants from seed we had gathered or ordered from wildflower societies. If we had enough in pots we could divide them up and start new plants that way.

If you want to plant wildflowers at home, read up on the plant and put it in where you guess it will be happy. Don't be surprised if it moves on you. Loosen up the soil, and mix in naturally-occurring things like peat moss and rotted leaves or weed-free compost. Bone meal is good fertilizer for wildflowers. Avoid barnyard manures that are probably full of weed seed.

Woodland wildflowers grow up and bloom before the leaves come out on the trees. They combine well with ferns which cover the ground after they are finished. I liked my planting centred around a hollow log that I dragged in with my tractor. Wetland and meadow wildflowers almost always like full sun, or close to it, and combine well with clump-forming grasses.

Once you are hooked, wildflower gardening is habit-forming and addictive, so beware. In contrast to the understated, God-given beauty of wildflowers, man-made hybrids begin to look pretty awkward. Somewhat like the difference between a doe and a cow.

Bruce Partridge

Vegetable gardening

Growing one's own food has appeal to old and young alike. The prospect of sowing seeds and harvesting well-grown, uncontaminated vegetables of your own is almost irresistible. Even city dwellers hopelessly trapped in high rise apartments are not exempt. There are few who don't put a pot of tomatoes on the deck or herbs on the windowsill. I believe that gardening is an inborn urge of human beings, going far back into the mists of time. Today, with most produce grown in other lands by nameless mega-farmers, the incentive is even stronger.

If there is a little piece of ground where you live that gets a fair bit of sun, you can be in business. During times of war and famine, people dug up yards and vacant lots in major cities and turned them to growing food. Why not? A well-grown vegetable garden not only provides nourishing food but is just as attractive as flowers and shrubs. Even in these peaceful times it makes sense.

There is really nothing more basic than putting seeds in the ground and watching them grow. The sun

will warm them and the rain will wet them and they will grow. That is their purpose in life, and they are not to be denied. The key words here, though, are the sun and the ground. To grow really well, vegetables need maximum sun, and soil that is not packed as hard as iron. The rain will wet the seeds, or they can be wet by the gardener, but the soil has to be right.

Forget for now whatever you have heard about nutrients that ought to be in the soil. These are of secondary importance. A seed will germinate with or without nutrients. The important thing is that the soil is loose to at least the depth of a shovel and mixed with organic matter to keep it that way.

Clay soils, such as we have in Northern Nova Scotia and Cape Breton, may be loosened up, but without organic matter they will settle and pack hard again when it rains. The life-giving rain either runs off or is trapped in the clay, where it becomes stagnant and actually suffocates and kills seeds. Adding quantities of organic matter in the form of animal manures, compost, rotted leaves or hay, seaweed, peat moss, grass clippings, or even sawdust, promotes drainage and prevents the clay from sticking together again. It's kind of like what happens to your bubblegum if you eat potato chips at the same time.

All the forms of organic matter I mentioned will loosen up the clay and—with the exceptions of peat moss or sawdust—supply many of those soil nutrients I told you to forget about earlier. Using peat moss or sawdust as a soil amendment just means you will have to augment with some other form of fertilizer.

If you are one of the uncommon few who actually garden in gravelly or sandy soil, organic matter is still the ticket. It captures moisture and prevents these soils from being too dry. If you have hit the jackpot and garden in fertile loam, you will still have to add organic matter to keep it that way.

This is nothing new. Organic matter in all its forms is the foundation of gardening and agriculture since prehistoric times and is the basis of fertility in all natural ecosystems.

An often misunderstood or unknown fact about fertile soil is that, besides water and nutrients, it has to contain air. A soil in good tilth, or in good heart, as they say, is by definition loose and automatically holds air in small open spaces, or pores. We all know that the leaves of the plant take in carbon dioxide and give off oxygen. Not everyone knows that the roots of plants do just the opposite. In order for roots to grow, they need to take oxygen out of the soil pores and expel carbon dioxide back in. They are truly breathing underground.

All this discussion is to point out that whether you are a beginning gardener or a pro, start by loosening up your ground.

Now, about those nutrients. All plants do indeed require a certain level of soil fertility to grow well. If any essential nutrients are seriously lacking, plants will be unhealthy. Vegetables are the worst. They need to complete their entire life cycle in one short summer, and should be growing at maximum speed with nothing to slow them down. This is why good vegetable gardens have to be especially fertile.

As I pointed out, a high level of organic matter in a soil contributes greatly to its fertility, and is always important. Organic matter is decomposable material and contains balanced levels of nutrients which it releases slowly into the soil as it rots. You can maintain a high level of fertility in the garden by regular additions of organic materials alone. This, along with no synthetic pesticides, is the basis of organic gardening. It does, however, take a few years to build up soil fertility with organic material alone.

Early in the twentieth century, scientists identified the three principal nutrients that plants required for best growth. These are nitrogen (N), phosphorus (P), and potassium (K). Growing plants take up N, P, and K in unusually large quantities and consequently most agricultural soils are lacking some or all of these. Of the three, nitrogen disappears from the soil most quickly so almost all soils are deficient in nitrogen.

After World War II, agricultural fertilizers containing various ratios of N, P, and K, mined from the earth or extracted from crude oil and converted into compounds taken up by plants, began to be available in bulk. When farmers applied these fertilizers to agricultural crops around the world, results were astounding. Yields increased unbelievably and it seemed as if there could never be a shortage of food on the planet again. This was the "Green Revolution".

Time has burst the bubble of euphoria and proven that overuse of N,P and K fertilizers harms the soil by burning up organic matter and leads to shortages of other essential nutrients, but...they can still be useful if you use them in tandem with quantities of organic matter, and you can find them at any garden centre, feed store or hardware store across the land. They are to this day widely used in agriculture—ideally combined with animal manures.

Chemical fertilizers are not poisonous, and you can use them in the home garden as a shortcut to quickly boost soil fertility. From then on you can maintain fertility with organic fertilizers. This might get you ahead a year or two—if you choose—instead of waiting for organic material to kick in.

Now, if you've got the soil loosened up and fertilized, go get some seeds. If you wait until the soil warms up a bit they should come right up. Peas, broad beans, all greens (lettuce, spinach, etc.), all root vegetables (carrots, parsnips, beets, turnips, salsify, etc.), and cole crops (broccoli, cauliflower, cabbage, kale, Brussels sprouts, kohlrabi, and so on) can be sown or set out as transplants in May. You can likewise set out onions as started plants or sets. A light frost won't hurt any of these.

You can plant potatoes in May, but a frost will kill them back to the ground if they are up, so you might have to cover them on a frosty night. If they are hit by frost they will re-grow, but it doesn't do them any good.

Don't plant the warm-season vegetables until the soil is nicely warmed up, which is usually the very last of May or first of June at the earliest. These include cucumbers, pumpkins, squash, corn, bush beans and pole beans. If you plant them before this, they take forever to come up, germinate unevenly, and may rot in the ground. It's better to wait.

Tomatoes, peppers and eggplant are warmth-loving vegetables that gardeners almost always set out as transplants after about the middle of June, when there is very little likelihood of a frost. You have to be alert, though, for a few weeks and cover them on a cold night. These are generally the last crops to go in the garden and by now you'll probably have to start hoeing weeds.

Insects will be next. They don't wait very long. You will almost certainly get to know the striped cucumber beetle and the cabbage worm. The cucumber beetle is tiny and striped yellow and black and gathers in hordes to shred the leaves of pumpkins, squash and cucumber as they try to get going. I start my plants indoors in 4" pots, then set them out when the weather is warm. Right away I cover each plant with a square of white row cover fabric held down with four little rocks. This keeps the beetles off them. When the plants are growing well and pushing up the fabric, I take it off. By then the plants are growing fast enough that the beetle can't do them much harm.

The cabbage worm is green like the cabbage and hard to see. If I see them I squash them with my fingers (this is guaranteed to kill any bug). Once I see white butterflies flitting around the garden I begin to spray all the cole crops with BtK insecticide every couple of weeks. BtK is a biological insecticide—a bacterium—that kills only the larvae of moths and butterflies. This includes almost all caterpillars and the cabbage worm, which is the larva of that white butterfly. It is approved for organic gardening and isn't harmful to people or animals.

The Colorado potato beetle is a scourge on potato plants and has wandered far from Colorado to everywhere in the world that potatoes are grown. If you are lucky, you won't find it on your potatoes, but most of us do. It takes two forms: the adult is a medium sized, striped, hard-shelled beetle. It is light in colour and quite visible from a distance. Larvae are soft and reddish, occur in masses and can be very tiny at first. If you overlook or ignore adults or larvae, you will quickly have an insect explosion on your hands and your potato plants will be devoured. I know of no effective insecticides for control of potato beetles that can be sold to home gardeners.

Potatoes are my favourite crop—along with onions—and I patrol my rows at least once a day, searching for potato beetle in either of its forms. I wear gloves, and if I find clusters of small larvae I just smear them to death. Larger larvae and adults I pick off and drop in a tin half-full of soapy water, then pour them out on the driveway when I am finished and smash them with my boot. We tried feeding them to the chickens, which relish most insects, but they won't eat potato bugs.

Slugs and snails are not insects but can really chew up the garden—especially later in the summer. They eat almost everything but are fondest of leafy vegetables. You might not see them in the daytime—they hide when you are awake but feed at night. If big ragged holes are appearing in your lettuces or cabbage and you can't find the cause, go out at night with a flashlight and you probably will. Slugs can also graze down a whole row of emerging lettuce or carrots early in the season.

Garden centres sell slug baits and traps that work quite well if used as directed. You can discourage slugs by dusting plants with diatomaceous earth, or you can go out at night with gloves and a flashlight and pick them off by hand. Drop them in a can half full of soapy water: it seems to do them in.

Garden mulches—particularly hay or straw—which are wonderful in the garden to hold moisture and keep down weeds, are unfortunately beloved by slugs and snails. They relish the dampness underneath to hide in and breed, and they come out at night to feed. If things get bad, you can flip your mulch over during the daytime and kill any slugs or slug eggs (look like transparent caviar) that you find. Leave old boards or cut-off cabbage leaves lying around the garden. Slugs will hide under them in the daytime, and they can be turned over and the slugs done away with.

Keep your calves out of your turnips.

You are almost certain to discover other troublesome garden pests I haven't mentioned, but the important thing is just to enjoy your garden. Wander through the garden in the evening with a beer or glass of wine and observe how everything is doing. This way you will discover and identify any problems before they get out of hand.

I want to make sure that I haven't made the vegetable garden sound too daunting. It really is the most basic, universal and understandable form of gardening. With a little bit of work and very little expense, you can be eating better vegetables than the Queen.

Considering the potential rewards, the work really isn't work at all, and you will almost certainly have satisfying results even with your first garden. You will get smarter, and your garden will get better every year, though perfection typically hovers just out of reach. I have been gardening for 45 years and haven't had the perfect garden yet. There is always something that doesn't grow the way it should.

That is what makes vegetable gardening so addictive, though—you always get another chance next year.

Bruce Partridge

Starting seeds

Human civilization would never have taken place without the seed. Virtually every plant we eat was domesticated and brought into cultivation by ancient peoples long before recorded history. The domesticated grains—particularly wheat, corn and rice—enabled the growth of thriving civilizations in ancient times, and sustain us to this day.

There is nothing more human than starting seeds, and in Spring it is impossible to resist checking the seed flats two or three times a day. At Pleasant Valley Nurseries we started lots of seeds, and never tired of it.

Nothing has changed since ancient times. All a seed needs to germinate and grow is the correct balance of warmth, moisture, and light. Containers and trays used for starting seeds should always have holes in the bottom to let excess water drain. Beginners tend to water too much. It's usually worthwhile to pre-moisten the growing mix in a bucket or tray by working water in with the hands. Only mix in enough water to bring the soil to about the dampness of a well-wrung-out towel. Then fill the planting trays and put in the seeds. Water the tray once after planting and let it drain. Cover it with a transparent cover or sheet of clear plastic. That should hold it until the seeds come up.

Finding a good, warm place to set the tray is of paramount importance. Seeds must germinate quickly and grow strongly to develop into good plants. The very best seed-starting situation is heat that comes up from the bottom. Commercial seed-starting trays are available with a heating pad to set the tray on. This is set at a temperature of about 25°C. A sunny warm windowsill or a greenhouse or a warm sunroom is ideal, but you can usually find other spots in the house to set a tray.

At home, we sometimes put a tray or two in the oven of our propane range with the heat off. The pilot light keeps the temperature just right. Sometimes the top of a refrigerator stays warm, or the top of some other electrical appliance, or a furnace duct or a radiator. Just be sure to check the trays often and get them into the light as soon as seedlings break the surface.

Besides the oven, we use a system of two two-bulb 48" fluorescent light fixtures, one above the other. They are set up on bricks or wooden blocks so that they are 3 or 4 inches above the seed flat. This is close enough that the heat of the bulbs warms the seeds. Both fixtures have racks on top where we can place additional seed trays to catch heat rising off the bulbs.

Immediately upon germination, light becomes paramount. A day or two of insufficient light causes seedlings to stretch, becoming so leggy and weak they may never recover. To forestall this situation, keep sprouted trays under the fluorescent bulbs, which you lift higher as the plants grow. We try to keep the lights just a couple of inches above the tops of the plants. As we run out of room under the lights, we move our seedlings to a small greenhouse outside, or to a sunny windowsill, until planting.

Seed trays under flourescent lights.

Growing seedlings is a matter of manipulating the three requirements to get the results you want. If the plants are growing tall and spindly, they need less heat and more light. If they are slow, they need more heat. If they are pale and unhealthy-looking, fertilize them with a water-soluble fertilizer.

This brings us to the subject of water. Don't water seedlings until they are just about to wilt. If the soil in the tray is not dry on top, leave it alone. Watering too frequently keeps the soil too cold and too wet, slowing growth and making seedlings susceptible to rot.

Don't worry: you will soon catch on to watering and everything else there is to know. I fear this old man is probably making things too complicated. Starting seeds really is so simple a child can do it. If you don't get it right the first try, you certainly will on the second.

Flowers and vegetables are not the only things that you can grow from seed. You can start almost any tree or shrub for which you can find seeds that way, as well as many perennials and wildflowers.

It becomes very interesting to gather seeds from the wild and try to grow them at home. Trees from seed grow much more rapidly than you would expect. A tree grown from seed will only be two or three years behind one that you bought from the garden centre, and may eventually catch it and pass it up because a seedling tree is more vigorous.

There is something you must realize, though. In Northern climates, seed ripened in Fall and dropping to the ground must not germinate until Spring—even if the weather is still warm. If a seed germinated as soon as it fell, winter would kill it. Northern plants produce seeds that have to go through a cold period (such as winter) for at least two or three months before they will germinate. This cold period also has to be damp—just like the ground in winter. Simply putting dry seed in the fridge doesn't work.

Plant seed gathered in the Fall in a seedbed outside right away. It will get its damp-cold treatment the way nature intended and germinate next Spring. This works well for large seeds like maple, oak, horse chestnut or nuts. If you know where you want the tree, you can put the seed in place and never have to move it. Or you can plant in a seed bed outside and transplant after a year.

When planting seeds outdoors, it is advisable to fasten down a piece of wire-mesh hardware cloth over them to ward off mice and squirrels. Alternatively, you can plant seed in trays and leave the trays outside for the winter, also covered, to germinate in the Spring. You can also stack trays of seeds for a couple of months in a root cellar or similar place where it doesn't quite freeze. This will satisfy the cold treatment. Then take these trays in where it is warm and bright, to germinate the seeds well before Spring.

Bruce Partridge

A last technique that works well is to mix a handful of seeds with a handful or two of damp but wrung-out peat moss in a jar or plastic bag and close it up. Keep these in the fridge for a couple of months. Check them from time to time to make sure they aren't germinating in the dark. After a couple of months—or sooner if they are already germinating—transfer them into flats and bring them into the light and warmth where they will grow.

Gathering and growing seeds of hardy plants costs very little and can yield lots of plants and lots of pleasure.

Saving seeds

Saving small quantities of seed to plant next summer's garden is satisfying and only makes sense. Seed is expensive and you might as well save money. Also, your seed will be fresh and will germinate quickly, and you can take seed from the nicest specimens and gradually improve your strain. Purchased seed is too often several years old when you get it, and germinates slowly or not at all. And then there is the problem of hybrid seed.

Hybrid seed for vegetable crops first began to show up in the 1950s, starting, I believe, with field crops and corn. Only large seed companies—often owned by chemical or petroleum corporations—can produce hybrid vegetable seed. It is necessary to maintain two true-breeding strains of the vegetable, which are then crossed (pollen from one strain fertilizing the flowers of the other), and grown to maturity. Companies do this on a huge scale, with ripened seed harvested by powerful machinery. Harvested seed is sold to seed sellers all over the world who sell it in bulk to farmers or in small packages to us. It may be a couple of years old by the time we get it.

Hybrid seed has become a fetish, and seed companies would have you believe that you are backwards and ignorant if you don't get on board. If you *do* get on board, you are stuck buying seed every year because you can't produce your own and hybrid vegetables don't breed true—meaning you can't save seed for next year. They've got you over a barrel.

Non-hybrid strains of vegetables are termed open-pollinated. If you save and plant seeds from these, the crop will be the same every year. The hybrid vegetables have become so prevalent that most open-pollinated varieties that we know and love are now called "heritage varieties". Hybrids started with corn, then came tomatoes and peppers and squash, then onions, and before we knew it there was hybrid celery and carrots and even beets. As far as I know there is no hybrid turnip. Not glamorous enough.

There is a phenomenon known as hybrid vigour, which means the hybrid cross produces a bigger, stronger plant and larger fruit than either of the parents. It's hard to argue with the results achieved with corn. Ears of open-pollinated corn, such as Golden Bantam, though tasty, are a bit on the small side. Hybrid everything else, though, doesn't impress me. We have all the good, open-pollinated varieties we need.

Some garden seed is very easy to harvest, some not so much. The easiest are those that produce large seeds and don't cross with other nearby strains. Peas and beans top the list. Leave dry beans growing until the plants begin to yellow in the Fall, and then harvest all the beans at once. I pull up the plants, pods and all, tie them in bundles and hang them under shelter to dry. Early in the winter, when I have time, I pull the pods off the vines, dry them indoors and shell them out while I listen to the radio.

Green beans and peas are more complicated because often I pick them all and forget to save any for seed. It's a good idea to deliberately leave one end of the row unpicked until pods dry up and the seed is ripe.

Tomatoes and their relatives are easy, too, and don't cross with one another. This includes the tomatoes, peppers, eggplants, and oddities such as ground cherry. Just scoop the seeds out of a ripe fruit and rub them through a strainer to separate seeds from pulp.

Lettuces also do not cross with one another and come true from seed. I have never heard of a hybrid lettuce. Lettuce is in the same family as dandelion, and harvesting seed is interesting. If you allow the lettuce to bolt and leave it alone, it will grow tall and produce heads of small yellow flowers. The flowers eventually dry up and leave little tufts of fluff like dandelion fluff. If you pinch the bit of fluff and pull it loose, you will find a few lettuce seeds attached at the bottom. It is somewhat tedious to harvest much lettuce seed, but you don't need much. It takes some work to separate the seed from the fluff, but you can do it by rubbing it through a screen. If the seed comes out mixed with ground-up fluff, don't worry. You just sow it all in the row together and it helps to avoid seeding too heavily.

Now things get more complicated. Pumpkins, squash, and melon seeds are very easy to harvest just by saving some when you are cleaning out the seed cavity for cooking. Save cucumber seed by leaving the fruit on the vine until it turns yellow, then extracting and drying the seeds.

The trouble is, bees pollinate all these vegetables, which will interbreed and produce seed that is all mixed up. Pumpkins will cross with some squash and different varieties of squash will cross with each other if they belong to the same family. There are three families of squash, I believe. Fortunately, squash from different families will not cross with each other, and this can be the solution.

I plant one variety from the first family, usually buttercup; one variety from the second family, butternut; and one from the third family, either acorn or delicata. None of these will cross across the family lines and I can save seed from all of them.

I keep my pumpkins and zucchinis as far away from the squashes as I can because I don't know what they cross with, and I only plant one variety of cucumber. If you are determined to plant a variety of different squashes and save seed, it is possible to pollinate a flower by hand and mark that fruit for seed.

Many vegetables are biennial, blooming and producing seed in their second year. Carrots, for instance, grow the nice orange carrot the first year, and do not bloom and produce seed unless you leave the root in the ground over the winter to sprout up in the Spring. Onions, parsnips and turnips behave the same way. It is tricky to gather seed from biennials, but it can be done. I have grown seed from all four by picking out the best specimens when I was harvesting in the Fall, potting them up, and keeping them in a root cellar until Spring.

Make sure you have two or three in a pot for cross-pollination. Brought outside in early Spring, they sprout, shoot up and bloom, and eventually ripen seed. Turnips are easy, but onions seem to be pollinated by flies which don't do a very good job and it may be necessary to pollinate them by hand.

Parsnips and carrots are a special case. They sprout up readily outside, but so do wild carrots (Queen Anne's lace), and wild parsnips. These will cross with the tame vegetables and spoil the seed. My solution was to move the pots of parsnip and carrots into a greenhouse very early in the Spring so that when I finally put them out they were almost blooming and well ahead of the wild ones.

Almost all members of the cabbage family, except for broccoli, are also biennial, sprouting up, blooming, and producing seed in the second year. I have never saved seed from cabbage, cauliflower, or Brussels sprouts, but broccoli will produce seed if you let some of the earliest florets bloom and produce seed capsules. Beware, though: it is difficult these days to find open-pollinated broccoli.

Dry any seed you save well, and store it in bottles or small plastic or paper bags somewhere cool and dry. Virtually any seed you harvest yourself will be viable for two or three years, so you don't need to gather everything every year.

Good luck, you will learn quickly by doing. Down with hybrids!

Bruce Partridge

Lawns

Just about any property owner will sooner or later want to put in a lawn, or at least patch one up. At the garden centre, new house owners were often the first customers in the Spring, desperate for lawn seed and fertilizer after walking on boards over the mud all winter. Construction is never complete until there is grass.

How lucky we are that there is such a thing as grass—a plant that can be mowed and take heavy traffic without any lasting harm. Other plants would be killed or trampled into mush. Grass forms a heavy sod with a mass of roots that protects soil from erosion. Unlike other plants, its growing points are at the base rather than the tips, so after you mow it, it comes right back. Grass is good-looking and easy to maintain, and around some buildings it's all you need.

In our climate, at the right time of year, seeding grass is almost a sure thing. Good lawn seed mixtures—most predominantly Kentucky bluegrass—are available nearly everywhere. If the spot is reasonably sunny, bluegrass will give you a first-rate lawn. In shade, it might be a good idea to purchase a seed mixture formulated with species that do better in the shade.

A lawn started from seed requires half the summer before it is tough enough to really use, however. Some owners of new construction choose to go with sods, which you can purchase in rolls, or as mats like pieces of carpet stacked on a pallet, which you then lay out over the ground. Sods are expensive, and sometimes hard to find, but you can install them rapidly. As long as the weather is not too dry, or if you can water the sods until they root, you have an instant lawn.

Sods hide the ground, and look good right away. Unfortunately, the temptation is to simply smooth out the construction mess with a machine and cover it with sod. A lawn, be it seeded or sodded, will not look good for long unless you prepare the soil adequately beforehand. Adequate preparation involves loosening up the soil where possible, or else adding a good layer of fresh loose topsoil, raking, liming and fertilizing.

Ground around new construction is generally cleaned up and contoured with a machine. Ideally, it is shaped with gentle slopes and contours that will be easy to mow and allow rainwater to flow away without getting trapped in puddles. At every stage, the objective is to minimize soil compaction by not working or running over the soil any more than necessary. Today, most of this work is done with the excavator, which is easier on the soil than the bulldozer. The excavator can back his way out of the property, loosening up and shaping the soil as he goes. If it is known where trees will be planted in the future, he can loosen up the soil especially deeply in those spots. Two feet would be about right.

If the soil is dry and loose—which is asking a lot—after the machine is gone, and if no topsoil is to be spread, you can lime and rake the ground. Limestone "sweetens" the soil—makes it less acid, in other words—and makes for a healthier lawn. If topsoil has been saved or has been purchased, spread it first. Ideally, do this in dry weather with a light machine.

Now the limestone goes on. Spread it before raking, because the more it is worked in the better. Agricultural limestone is dusty and dirty but won't burn anything. It comes most often in 20 or 25 kilo bags. On the bag it says 2 bags for 1000 square feet of area, so unless you have a soil test that disagrees with this, that is what you use. If you don't have a spreader, throw the limestone with a shovel evenly over the area, trying to get some everywhere. A perfect job is not necessary. You will spread it all around while raking.

The object of raking is not to remove rocks, and it shouldn't be a back-breaking job. The object of raking is to smooth out rough spots left by the machines and to fine-tune the contours—filling in hollows so that rainwater runs off and doesn't form big puddles anywhere. You can locate low spots by crouching down and sighting as well as possible across the surface of the ground. Rake soil from high spots into hollows to even them up. Sometimes it is useful to skim soil into a wheelbarrow with a shovel to move a larger volume and save raking. You don't need to take away stones smaller than your fist. Just rake them into the hollows and tamp them flat. Flick a little finer material over them and grass will grow right over top. We often raked out large areas of rocky ground without removing anything.

LAWNSEED

Using **Good Quality Seed** is the secret.
Our Canada #1 Lawn Mix, 'Greenfast', is the best all-around lawnseed your money can buy. It's especially blended for our Nova Scotia climate and soil conditions.
It has proven to be superior to any other seed mix ever sold by us. In fact, it's so good that a **money-back guarantee** comes with it.

NOTE: Anyone purchasing seed from our store is eligible to make use of our **spreader, seeder** and **roller.**

50% Kentucy Bluegrass
20% Highlight Chewing Fesque
20% Creeping Red Fesque
10% Annual Ryegrass

Immediately after raking, before the ground has had a chance to settle and cake, is the time to spread fertilizer and seed. It doesn't matter which goes first—maybe the seed so that it gets pressed a bit into the soil by foot traffic. Spread seed as evenly as you can either by hand or with a light cyclone spreader. Those are the ones with a bucket for the seed and a spinning disk underneath to spread the seed. A drop spreader from which seed trickles out underneath works even better, but is slower. It is not necessary to put seed down too heavily—follow the guidelines on the bag for coverage.

If the ground is still soft and loose, you can follow seeding by rolling with a heavy roller to press it into the ground. If there is no roller, or if the soil is not so soft or is stony, quickly rake over the area with the back of a fan rake. This will brush some soil over the seed but won't move it all around. It is quite imperative that seed be in good contact with the soil, and not perched up high and dry on the rocks and clods.

You can spread fertilizer right over the seed without hurting it. Usually it is granular fertilizer with a high middle number (phosphorus) such as 12-18-12 or 8-16-8, or old-fashioned 6-12-12. The fertilizer gives germinating grass seed what it needs to grow strongly and become established fast. If the area is not too large, it is worth the extra money to buy fertilizer that is formulated with slow-release nitrogen, which will feed the grass for several months. You can quickly spread granular fertilizer with the cyclone spreader and roll or lightly rake the ground to cover the seed, if this hasn't been done already. If you are lucky enough to have a big pile of manure or compost you can dispense with the granular fertilizer and cover the seed with that.

If the property is to be sodded, prepare the ground as if for seed before putting the sods in place. It is also becoming very common to have lawns started by hydro-seeding. In this case, the ground is sprayed with an emulsion of paper pulp, seed and fertilizer. This works very well, but you should still prepare the ground in advance as if for seed, though maybe omitting the fertilizer. If, for some reason, there has been a delay between raking and seeding and the ground has hardened up, I have found it successful to spread the fertilizer and seed, and then run over the area with a rototiller set to a depth of one or two inches to bury the seed.

At Pleasant Valley Nurseries, any lawn seeding jobs that failed were invariably due to seed insufficiently covered on dry hard ground, and dry weather.

Ideally, put in a lawn during the seasons of the year when the weather is warm but not dry. Mid-summer is usually out. The best bet is Spring until mid-June or Fall after the end of August. Grass will germinate at any temperature above freezing, but it is much faster in warm weather. Grass comes up quickly when seeded in Fall but you must seed early enough that grass is mature enough to make it through winter. End of September is probably the cut-off.

Laying sod.

Sod and hydro-seeding are slightly less weather dependent than seed alone, but either one can still dry up in hot dry weather. Of course, if it is possible to water until grass is established, you can put in a lawns during any month that the weather is warm.

Now that lawn herbicides have largely been taken off the market —and rightly so—a weed-free lawn is a virtual impossibility. It may be necessary to learn to appreciate dandelions and creeping Charlie. Scientifically, a lawn that is mixed with weeds is ecologically more diverse and more resistant to infestation by insects than grass is alone.

By the way, if you have just seeded a new lawn and everything comes up in horrible-looking weeds, do not despair. This is an indication that the soil is good and the grass will be in there somewhere. Those weeds are annual weeds that will disappear once you begin to mow.

Grass is most healthy and most resistant to weeds and insects if it is not mowed too short. Lawns are best kept between 2.5 and 4 inches high, and not allowed to get much over 4 inches before you mow again. If the lawn looks pale, it would be good to put on lawn fertilizer or, better yet, a layer of manure or compost, and to apply limestone every few years.

A very good way to make fertilizer unnecessary is to mix white clover seed into the lawn seed when seeding. You may also sprinkle white clover seed into an existing lawn. White clover forms a rather tough low sod itself, which intermingles with the grass to help exclude undesirable weeds. Most importantly, white clover takes nitrogen from the air—as do all legumes—and puts it in the soil where it serves to fertilize the grass and keep it healthy.

Lawns are almost universal around homes and other buildings in Nova Scotia and may vary in extent from a small parcel to acres. There is almost nothing else you can use, or that is more attractive, to cover torn-up soil from construction. Beyond this, you may have, or wish to have, an extra expanse of lawn for recreation or to enhance the property. Think twice, though, before you get rid of native vegetation to make more lawn.

Along the seashore above the Northumberland Strait, where wind and winter blizzards come straight off the salt water, a landscape of densely growing, intertwined woody shrubbery, including alder, wild rose, serviceberry, chokecherry, bayberry, winterberry, chokeberry, and others, interspersed with windswept birches and spruce, is found. This vegetation is much older than it looks and is stable and well-established. In general it is low—less than the height of a man—and shelters itself from the wind. It includes species tolerant of salt spray, and the dense growth prevents any one plant from bearing the brunt. A single tree, growing in this location, would be doomed.

Soil is thin, sour and vulnerable along these bluffs, and the dense vegetation protects it from erosion. Best of all, the shrubbery is beautiful. Almost everything blooms and has colourful berries in the Fall. You can gather many of these, and they are a valuable food for wildlife. Fall colour is outstanding. Why would you trade this for grass?

People do it, though. It takes a very short time to thoughtlessly bulldoze and push this perfect plant community over the bank, along with the scanty topsoil. Then the property owner calls Pleasant Valley Nurseries out to have a look at the ugly, wet mud that is left and estimate a price to plant it all in grass, or, even more absurdly, to put in a fruit orchard or maple trees. Well, the landowner can spend a million dollars or two, and never have a fruit orchard or maple trees, and will not see the land restored in their lifetime. This for a few acres of soggy grass.

Forest land is vulnerable, too. You can't take away the outside of a nice stand of spruce without exposing the naked trunks of the trees behind, predisposing the whole stand to blow down in an ugly tangle. Also, you can't clear the native vegetation from around mature hardwoods to make room for grass. The trees and the understory go together. Why interfere?

Though lawns certainly are good-looking and useful where we need them, I think we Nova Scotians could temper our love affair with grass sometimes and let native plant communities look after things.

Invasive plants

Any long-time gardener will have had an encounter with invasive plants. They want to take over the garden or flower bed and crowd everything else out. Experience teaches, for the most part, which plants to avoid, but they can take beginners by surprise.

My definition of an invasive is any plant that someone gives you for free. If they have enough to give away, watch out! Or they could be aggressive weeds from vacant lots or farm fields that invade your property. You may have acquired them unwittingly in a load of topsoil or manure, or dug up a piece because it is pretty.

Don't worry, I have done all these things. The worst invasive plants are perennials that spread from creeping underground roots or rhizomes—every piece of which can start a new plant. Some can spread from seed as well.

Invasiveness can run the gamut from a mild nuisance to a horrid plague. Certain violets and forget-me-nots are enthusiastic spreaders, but are low and pretty and can't be taken too seriously. At the other end of the spectrum are the noxious brutes like Japanese knotweed and stinging nettle which will most certainly outlive the human race. If these get started on your property, they are almost impossible to beat and can make your property difficult to sell. The important thing is to be attentive and never let them get started in the first place.

Beware, as I said, of plants offered for free. Find out what it is if you don't know, and get advice from experienced gardeners. If you bring home manure or topsoil to use in your garden and see numerous chunks of root, or pieces of plants all of the same type—watch out. Don't use it until you find out what those mysteries are. Take a sample to a gardener or let them grow in the pile until someone can identify them. Also, don't dig up and take home plants that you know nothing about.

Bruce Partridge

I have had plenty of experience with invasive plants myself, living in the middle of old farmland as I do. I also rented out my house and garden more than once and came back to deal with invasives that the renters had started. And yes, I was far too often guilty of accepting plant gifts from my friends and fellow gardeners.

Here is a list of plants to beware of that I have compiled from my own experience and that of my friends, starting with the worst.

The Worst

Japanese knotweed. *Polygonatum cuspidatum*

This nightmare is also called elephant ear or sometimes bamboo. The stems are hollow and as tall as a grownup human. The leaves are very large near the base, and smaller towards the tip. Knotweed grows in thickets, usually near water, but can grow anywhere. Thickets of knotweed are common from Cape Breton probably through to Yarmouth. There is a lot of it in the Halifax Public Gardens. Much of this knotweed has been planted unwittingly by property owners who thought it was pretty; but it spreads on its own, too, by thick underground rhizomes and seeds.

Don't let anyone give you this plant and don't dig any up yourself. It is really a world-wide scourge and in England you aren't allowed to sell a house if Japanese knotweed is growing on the property.

Stinging nettle. *Urtica dioica*

This plant is ugly and unremarkable in appearance, and can grow three or four feet high over large areas, overwhelming all other vegetation. It does occur naturally in Nova Scotia but the worst strains are the ones imported from Europe. They are more aggressive than the natives, and, as the name implies, can raise painful blisters if the leaves brush against bare skin. Why anyone would plant stinging nettle is a mystery to me, though it is promoted as a healthy tea and for animal fodder. I have seen seed companies selling the seed. Nettle spreads uncontrollably by underground roots and seed. Don't plant it! If you want nettle tea, get dried leaves from someone who is already overrun with it.

Bruce Partridge

Couch grass. *Agropyron repens*

If you do any gardening at all, you are almost certain to run into this one. Couch grass is an ordinary looking grass that can grow three or four feet high in good soil. It was introduced from Europe to stabilize railroad embankments and it can stabilize your garden beds just as happily. It spreads from tough, stringy, white underground rhizomes, any piece of which can grow into a new plant.

It is often found in loads of manure or topsoil as clumps of grass attached to tangles of these rhizomes. In the garden it grows into any bits of unoccupied ground it can find and insinuates itself into the roots of shrubs and perennials, where it is almost impossible to weed out. In a shrub bed it not only makes the planting look messy and unkempt, but it can crowd out perennials or low-growing garden plants such as strawberries. The only defence is to learn to recognize it and weed it out promptly, roots and all, before it can spread.

Borderline Hardy in 5b

Horseradish. *Armoracia rusticana*
I haven't had much experience with this one, but am told it can get away from you, especially in rich soil. It is grown to make a sauce for meat—which I like myself—but they say it should be grown in a bucket that it can't get out of.

Comfrey. *Symphytum officinale*

Unfortunately, this plant is pretty with its soft-looking leaves and blue flowers, and free, so it is very tempting for new gardeners. It is reputed to have some medicinal properties, but I'm not sure what they are. It spreads unstoppably by roots and seed once it gets going. I have seen formerly-nice vegetable gardens overrun with the stuff. Again, if you want comfrey leaves, get them from someone who has too much of it.

Goutweed. *Aegopodium podagraria*
Our house in St. Andrews was built in 1950, and the banks along the road and the drive, and much of the property, is smothered in goutweed. I'm sure we will never get rid of it and, at my age, I'm not even going to try. Fortunately, it is fairly attractive and doesn't grow too high—maybe two feet. Taller, vigorous trees and shrubs

may be able to cope with it, but it is almost impossible to start new ones. A fairly well-behaved variegated green and white leaved form of goutweed is sometimes sold at garden centres as a ground cover. It is the green-leaved form that is seriously invasive.

The trouble is that the variegated form can revert to the green-leaved one. Don't plant either one. In Guysborough County I have seen goutweed invading farm fields and growing even into the woods.

Creeping Bluebell. *Campanula rapunculoides*
This is another Jezebel that is pretty and tempting to dig up and plant. It is also very probable that someone will offer you some from their garden. It grows two feet high along untended fences and in waste areas and bears pretty blue flowers. It spreads uncontrollably by seed and rubber-band-like roots all through the soil. The roots cannot be dug up without breaking, and each piece left in the ground will re-grow. My daughter spent all Summer one

year fruitlessly trying to keep it under control in a garden she was tending for Alice Hoskins.

It is on the official 'invasive, do not plant' list of most states and provinces and even European countries. Stay clear of it.

Bad

Chinese Lanterns. *Physalis alkekengi*
Another plant that spreads underground from thick white roots and probably also from seed. It's an unattractive plant that can smother out nicer things. All it has going for it are the small papery, orange seed pods that resemble, well, Chinese lanterns. I had a personal battle with this one when it got in around shrubs where I wanted to plant better stuff. I eventually won by digging out all the plants I could, roots included, then checking every day for two summers to dig up anything sprouting from pieces I had missed. Needless to say, I was soon able to spot a Chinese lantern sprout from a mile away. We have since sold the property and the lanterns could very well be back by now. Chinese lanterns can grow out of control in good soil and smother out more delicate plants.

If you want to grow them, pick an untended bank or a brush pile or some waste ground where it doesn't matter if they spread

Dame's Rocket. *Hesperis matronalis*
This is another one I had an ongoing battle with at home. When we sold the place the score was still 0-0. Dame's rocket is sometimes called wild phlox. It resembles garden phlox, with attractive fra-

grant pink or purple or white flowers, and is naturalized along riverbanks in our area. A friend gave me plants and I put them in, thinking that since my place was high and dry and far from the river, they probably wouldn't even grow. They did, though, and were pretty so I left them alone for a few years. I ignored the fact that each summer they were producing thousands of seeds which were unobtrusively sprouting up everywhere.

The first year, seedlings are low and unnoticeable, but the next year they sprout up three or four feet high. Soon they were everywhere and crowding out my plantings of delicate wildflowers. I pulled up all I could find every Summer after they finished blooming but before they could set seed. Somehow, there were always just as many the next Summer. I only ever managed to keep even with them.

They might not be so pushy in your yard but I would advise you to leave them down by the river where they belong.

Burdock. *Arctium minus*
You will know this weed already if you have a horse or dog. It's that nasty burr that is so hard to get out of a tail or a tangled forelock. Burdock is a biennial that grows low the first year and looks like rhubarb. The second year it shoots up high with clusters of the burrs. They say that the fellow who invented Velcro learned it from burdock.

The best way I know of to get rid of it is to bend the second-year plant down to the ground with your foot and hold it there, then chop the root out with a grub hoe, getting as big a piece as you can. Do this while the burrs are still green and don't fall off too readily. Fortunately, these second year plants don't seem to sprout up again from roots left in the ground, as a dandelion would. I generally ignore first year burdocks, then chop them out the next year. Burn the plants or dump them where it doesn't matter if they come back to life.

The idea is to eliminate plants every year before they can produce seed. It takes a few years to get ahead.

Not so bad

Aluminum plant. *Lamiastrum galeobdolon*
This a creeping plant with metallic-looking leaves and yellow flowers and is universally sold in garden centres to plant in hanging baskets or as a ground cover in outdoor beds. I am including it as a plant to avoid because Henri has seen it get away and form large colonies in the nearby forest. It is tolerant of shade and can crowd out desirable native wildflowers.

Virginia creeper. *Parthenocissus quinquefolia*
Virginia creeper, with its glossy maple-like leaves and outstanding scarlet Fall colour, has a place in the landscape. That place is not among trees and shrubs, though, which it climbs and engulfs, bowing them over to the ground with its weight. It can climb the tallest tree, and can have a stem as thick as my wrist. It is also hard to get rid of. Confine Virginia creeper plantings to brush piles and fences or old buildings where its beauty can be appreciated and it can do no harm.

Jerusalem artichoke. *Helianthus tuberosus*
This is a tall sunflower native to North America, and can flower in the garden and look very nice. It produces a small, potato-like tuber that is said to be tasty and healthful. I'm going to give them a better try next summer. The tubers, though, can never all be removed from the ground and the ones you miss sprout up the next year. A patch can expand rapidly, especially in rich ground, and become a troublesome weed in garden beds where it doesn't belong.

If you plant Jerusalem artichokes, try to put them in an area of their own where you can mow the grass around them to keep them in place.

Mints. *Mentha* species
All the mints I know of can be pushy: peppermint, spearmint, apple mint, etc. If they go into a bed of good soil, they will come up

through other plants and are hard to eradicate. Plant them in spots that they can have for themselves and can't escape. They like damp areas and don't need especially good soil.

I am not including **annual weeds** in this list of invasive plants, even though they can be obnoxious and a big problem in the garden. Annuals, as the name implies, start over fresh every Spring, from seed. They invariably produce millions of seeds, are fast-growing, and can come up in the garden thick as grass.

On the plus side, the fact that annual weeds start from seed means they have to wait for the soil to warm up to get started, so they don't get a very early start. You can pull most of them out fairly easily if the soil is not too dry, and you can hoe or smother them under mulches such as hay or bark.

Some annual weeds are edible: lamb's quarters, *Chenopodium album,* is a delicious wild spinach.

Control

Control of the tough perennial invasives on this list is sometimes possible, but eradication usually is not. Keeping plants cut short by mowing or whipper-snipping will weaken them if you do it repeatedly. You can achieve control in some cases by covering the ground with black plastic, a layer of cardboard and hay, a thick layer of hay alone, or something similar to completely cut off sunlight. You will have to leave this covering in place all summer and it still may not kill the plants completely. It will probably, in any case, induce them to grow roots closer to the surface where they are more easily dug up.

Digging is my method. It starts with a thorough rooting up of the area with a shovel or garden fork to remove all the plants and roots that I can locate, This works best in damp soil after a rain. Then it's a question of close, almost-daily surveillance of the area to spot and remove any sprouts growing from bits of root that I missed. It is important to get under these sprouts with a trowel or spade and lift completely the piece of root the sprout is attached to.

Keep an eye on the spot next year, too. You will develop an eye for the quarry and spot any survivors. Once new sprouts seem to stop coming, it would be a good idea to spread a heavy mulch of hay or bark to discourage new weeds getting started. Using this program I have defeated couch grass and Chinese lanterns, though admittedly in rather small, easily-managed areas.

The heavyweights, particularly knotweed and nettle, have been, and are being (in the case of knotweed) controlled with chemical herbicides. Roundup (glyphosate) is the herbicide usually chosen. Glyphosate is not supposed to be harmful to people or animals and is used extensively in Europe and the U.S.A. Homeowners in Nova Scotia are not allowed, and *shouldn't* be allowed, to use herbicides at home, but glyphosate and a long list of other compounds are used here in forestry and agriculture.

Both Japanese knotweed and stinging nettle are on the noxious-plant list in Nova Scotia and if you are desperate enough you might report the infestation to the Department of Agriculture and see if they will spray. It takes repeated treatments over three to five years to control knotweed and a professional has to do it. Controlling nettles is not a whole lot easier and also requires a professional.

Both the timing and the concentration of herbicide are critical. Even so, spraying is unlikely to eradicate the problem, because invasives can work their way back into the treated area over time from plants that survived around the edges.

It goes without saying that the best way to control these invasives is to not plant them in the first place. But it may not be your fault they are on your property. Aggressive plants can appear on their own, or may have been planted by a previous tenant.

Try to find out what the plant is and what gardeners say about it. The internet is a big help in this. Watch for plants in the garden that are spreading too fast—growing underground or sprouting up from seed in places where they are not supposed to be. Take steps to get rid of them before they become a problem.

Bruce Partridge

Take heart, though. Gardening is almost by definition a process of working away on your hands and knees, digging out weeds and things you shouldn't have planted. I've been doing it for forty years, and God willing, I'll do it for a few more.

The back of the book

Bruce Partridge

Acknowledgements

I wish to thank Janette Fecteau, writer and astute editor who encouraged me and laughs at my jokes, and of course Mary, my wife and soul-mate, who laughs at most of my jokes. Henri Steeghs did some critical editing and is the source of all the best stories in the book. Phyllis, who knows me too well, was a valuable source of skepticism.

Bruce Partridge

About the author

Bruce Partridge was born in Salt Lake City, Utah, and raised in New Mexico. He was hooked on plants when required to make a plant collection for a botany class at Utah State University in 1965, and his goose was cooked after a boring summer job spent reading old issues of *Organic Farming and Gardening* instead of working.

Arriving in Antigonish, Nova Scotia in 1973, he soon had a homestead of his own, a diploma in horticulture, and the perfect job working for Pleasant Valley Nurseries, where he worked for 39 years.

He is now 73 years old and the father of four grown children. He lives in St. Andrews N.S., gardens, and shares his time with his wife, Mary, and his antique '72 Volkswagen Beetle.

www.ingramcontent.com/pod-product-compliance
Lightning Source LLC
Chambersburg PA
CBHW071412070526
44578CB00003B/561